HISTORY

—OF THE—

GRAFF ✻ FAMILY

—OF—

WESTMORELAND CO

BY PAUL GRAFF

PHILADELPHIA
1891

PREFACE.

In the centennial year, 1876, I began to make inquiry about the ancestry of the Graff and Baum families. I wrote to all my brothers and sisters in Pennsylvania, Ohio, Illinois, and to other friends in the State of Indiana. As they were not able to give a satisfactory account of the families I pursued my researches elsewhere. In the Spring of 1877, in company with my wife and daughter, I went abroad, traveling through Germany and stopping at Neuwied, on the Rhine, the place of my father's birth. After considerable inquiry we found a person who knew something about the family. We first went to the cemetery where we found the tombs of grandfather, Henry Graff, and a number of his children. We next visited the church of which grandfather had been a member for so many years. The minister who had charge of the Parish, brought out the records of the church, and to our great surprise we found the names and dates of the births and deaths of all the family. After visiting some cousins we found the name of Graff was extinct in the city of Neuweid. After returning to our homes in October, 1877, I continued my investigation, writing to the different members of the family again, and visiting them personally. Nearly all of them have since died. Now as I have exhausted all means of obtaining further light on our ancestry, by fourteen years of constant research, and writing over two hundred letters of inquiry, I will close in the hope that it may stimulate those who may read this biography to imitate these Christian fathers and mothers.

PAUL GRAFF.

History of the Graff Family.

THE earliest account we have is near the opening of the 17th century, when Jacob Graff lived at Grafenauer Hof Castle, near Mannheim, Germany. After this castle was destroyed in some of the wars, the family removed to Mannheim, and as far as known, he lived there until his death. As all the municipal and church records were destroyed it is not known whether his children were born at Grafenauer Castle or Mannheim. Many families of the same name are now living at the latter place.

Jacob Graff had three children at least. The eldest, born about 1726, came to America and settled near Lancaster, Pa. The second son, Henry, was born January 16th, 1736, was married February 21st, 1762, and died in 1802. The daughter Barbara was born May 31st, 1744, and married in 1767, to Nicolases Gramm. Their heirs are still living as small farmers near Neuwied, Germany. We also know of a Peter Graff, living on the Unkerhof, and married to Elizabeth Ellenberger. Their children are James Graff, born 1764, died November 15th, 1824; Daniel, born 1767 and died 1809, unmarried; Rhine Miller, time of birth and death unknown; and John, born ——, died 1828, at Freisenheim.

In the records of Lancaster Co., Pa., is an account of Sebastian Graff, who died in 1791. He was prominent

in the affairs of the city of Lancaster, and must have been the son of Jacob Graff, who came to America and settled near that place. In the same records are the names of Hans, Sebastian, George, Henry and John, who must have been sons of Sebastian. On his way to Germany in 1816, Henry Graff, son of John, of Westmoreland Co., was taken sick and remained with his cousin in Lancaster Co. until his recovery, when he returned to his father's home. From all the information we can gather they must have been descendants of this same Sebastian. Henry Graff, born 1736, made a trip to America while yet a young man, perhaps, with his brother Sebastian. After accumulating some means, he returned to Germany and married Mary Friedt, who was born August 10th, 1742, and died October 23d, 1817. They settled in Neuwied, Germany. He was a man of considerable note in church and state, a devoted Christian, and held the position of President or Elder in the Mennonite church for twenty-seven years. He was buried at Neuwied with his wife.

They had nine children as follows; [1818

John, (our father),	born 1763;	went to U. S. A., 1783, died,	
Paul,	born 1765,	died young, no account of death	
Catharine,	" 1767,	" " " " "	
Susannah,	" 1768,	" " " " " "	
Elizabeth,	" 1770,	" " " " " "	
Jacob,	" 1772,	died 1849,	at Neuwied.
Peter,	" 1775,	" 1842,	unmarried
Elizabeth,	" 1778,	" 1840	
Margaret,	" 1784,	" 1846	

Elizabeth, the eighth child, married Fred Herman who died August 13th, 1840 They had ten children two of which were still living near Neuwied, in 1888

Margaret, the ninth child, married George Vetter, who died in 1846 Their heirs are still living

Jacob, the sixth child married and had a number of children, but his family are all dead The name of Graff is extinct in Neuwied, as those bearing it are all dead John, the eldest son, came to America in 1783 with his uncle Wm Friedt, his mother's brother They landed in Philadelphia and went to Lancaster Co, where they spent several years with cousins. They afterwards decided to go further West, and travelled together through Dauphin, Juniata, Mifflin, Huntingdon, Blair and Cambria Counties Wm Friedt settled at Greensburg, the county seat of Westmoreland Co, where he resided until his death, March 9th, 1819, unmarried

John Graff settled six miles from the county seat, where he purchased a farm of 200 acres in 1792 and lived on it until his death, Dec 31st, 1818 at the age of 57 years His last words were "Jesus take me quickly" He was an active business man, strictly honest in all his dealings and successful in his undertakings He was modest and retiring in his manners, a kind and loving father, being very particular about the associates of his children and the books they read He was a member of the German Lutheran Church near Pleasant Unity, and months before he died spent much of his time in prayer.

In 1793, he married Barbara Baum, and their children were as follows

I	HENRY	born May 27th, 1794,	died Sept	9th, 1855
II	MARY,	" Sep 4th, 1795,	" Dec	4th, 1833
III	SARAH,	" May 3d, 1797,	" Sep	16th, 1850
IV	WILLIAM,	" Oct. 1st 1798,	" Nov	18th, 1882
V	JOHN,	" Aug 3d, 1800	" Jan	31st, 1885
VI	MARGARET,	" May 3d, 1802,	" Mar	24th, 1885
VII	JOSEPH,	" Oct 13th, 1804,	" Oct	13th 1804
VIII	ELIZABETH,	" Jan 7th 1807,	" May	10th, 1888
IX	PETER,	" May 27th, 1808,	" April	9th, 1890
X	JACOB	" Sep 5th, 1810,	" Dec	9th, 1886
XI	MATTHEW,	" Aug 23d, 1812		
XII	PAUL,	" May 31st, 1815		

His wife, Barbara Baum, was a descendant of the Waldensians, who suffered extreme hardships and persecutions on account of their faith

During the religious persecutions in France, our great grandfather, Mathias Baum, concluded, with other friends, to leave his native land, Alsace, and seek a more congenial country to live in He sailed from Rotterdam in the ship Alice, Hartly Cossack, Commander, and arrived in Philadelphia with his family September 3rd, 1743 Of his subsequent movements and death, we have no further information

Our grandfather, Frederick who was about fourteen years of age on his arrival, must have remained in Philadelphia a number of years, as our cousin Daniel Ringle said that our grandfather told him a short time

before his death in 1831, that he was a shipbuilder, and worked in a yard on the Delaware river (Mr Ringle was living in the State of Indiana, in 1886, at the age of eighty years on my last visit)

He must have been over twenty-one years of age when he and a family named Ullman concluded to go westward He may have been married to Barbara Ullman before leaving Philadelphia or shortly after They travelled through Chester, Lancaster and Cumberland counties, and partly through Franklin, locating near the Burnt Cabins in Path Valley The white squatters had built cabins to live in When notified by the government to leave, they burned these cabins lest the Indians who were trading and located in the valley in large numbers, should occupy them. Path Valley was named as the records of that period indicate, from the fact that the road was only a path for pack horses It was opened by the Indians, and used at that time by traders over the mountains. The path became known as Braddock's Road.

His children were born during his residence in the valley. The Indians became very troublesome and dangerous to live among. As grandfather was a favorite among them, he was often informed of their movements, and was thus enabled to provide for the safety of his family As the disturbances continued, and murders were committed, grandfather became alarmed and left the settlement He crossed the Juniata and Susquehanna rivers to Duncan's Island, and northward to

Sunbury, Northumberland Co., where we next hear of him. His family must have remained there for some time, as he left them until he could find a more suitable place to live He joined a party going north-westward In crossing the mountains he cut notches in the trees to mark the road so that his family might be able to follow him or he might find the way back We next hear of him at French Creek, Crawford Co He located on a farm of two hundred acres about two miles from Meadville as one of the earliest settlers He was absent from his family six months, and when they found him he had cleared some land and sowed grain. He made wooden troughs to hold milk and had a trough for churning butter in by the use of wooden paddles The family were several months in crossing the mountains, and met with many difficulties Trees were blown down, Indians were on the alert to rob or murder travellers, they were obliged to bury their goods on the way and use every precaution to prevent being murdered

Grandfather spoke about oil he had often dipped up with a feather and was good for many things. He spoke about being in Punxsutawny He was one of a party who took the first raft down French Creek and the Allegheny River to Pittsburg It was said that camp meetings were held on his farm The family evidently lived many years in the neighborhood of Meadville

The Baums were a quiet and peaceable family, but large and powerful men They were, however, great Indian fighters The Indians were numerous and gave

the settlers a great deal of trouble by committing raids, robberies and murders So there was need of constant vigilance A story is related of the Indians coming at one time in large numbers, when word was at once sent to the Baum family They immediately responded and were placed in the fort. The Indians advanced, whooping and howling, and as they neared the fort and found the Baums were in and around it, they quickly turned and retreated.

Our grandfather lived in Westmoreland and northwestern counties until 1816, being then over eighty-five years old He had accumulated quite a fortune for those days and gave to his three sons as follows

John, the eldest, who settled in St Joseph, Missouri, six thousand dollars. Frederick, who settled in Ohio, six thousand, and to Jonas, a farm near Waynesburg in Stark Co, Ohio, where his son now lives This was done with the understanding that they would furnish their parents with a comfortable home and support during their natural life But the ungrateful sons failed to provide for their aged parents The daughter, Barbara, our mother, who lived in Pennsylvania, hearing of their condition, arranged with her two sons William and Matthew, to have them brought from Ohio to her home at Pleasant Unity, six miles south of Greensburg, Westmoreland Co. This was done during the cold winter months of 1829, a distance of more than one hundred and fifty miles. A two horse wagon was used with a square box bed resting on the axle without springs, as

wagons were made in those days It was covered with muslin and furnished with plenty of straw, a feather bed and quilts to keep them warm As it became very cold after they started, large stones were heated and placed to their feet. The trip occupied more than two weeks Grandfather was about one hundred years old, and grandmother ninety-two. They remained only one year, as they became homesick and wished to return They were taken back and Mrs Ringle, a daughter, took charge of them until their death A few days before his death grandfather insisted on walking five miles to see his son Jonas This was too much for his strength, and not having enough vitality to rally from the exhaustion, he died in a few days This was in 1831, and his age one hundred and three years Grandmother lived four years longer and died in 1835 aged ninety-seven years. The children were as follows.

JOHN BAUM, emigrated to St Joseph, Missouri, and died there In 1886 some of his children were living in Indiana

FREDERICK,	married,		died in Ohio
JONAS,	"		" " " Stark Co
CATHARINE,	"	Michal,	" " Kentucky
SUSAN,	"	Barr,	" " Michigan
MARY,	"	Ringle,	" " Ohio
ELIZABETH,	"	Vanosten,	" " "
BARBARA			

Barbara was born in 1775, made captive in 1783, married to John Graff in 1793, and died March 12th, 1841. The place of her birth was near the Burnt Cabins

in Path Valley. It was a wilderness where Indians were lurking and seeking whom they might devour. She was captured while out in the woods, a short distance from home, and carried off several miles to their huts by a party of Indians. She would have been scalped and murdered, perhaps, had it not been for an old Indian who, when starving in the cold winter months, had received kindness from the family. On returning home in the evening he recognized the little nine year old girl and plead for her release. After considerable Indian talk he pinned up her clothes and told her to run for her life, and doing so she made her escape. She was a child of God early in life and lived with friends who were devoted followers of Christ. She loved to hear the word of God read and the prayers which were offered in his house. God spared her life through many hardships and narrow escapes for some wise purpose. At the age of eighteen she was married to John Graff in 1793 and became the mother of twelve children. Twenty-five years after her marriage she was left a widow with the care of a large farm and family. The children were all at home, and the three eldest sons assisted her in the management of affairs. She was a member of the United Brethren Church. Many incidents are related of her Christian life which show her to have been a devoted Christian. Among other conversations told by her son John was one shortly before her death, in which she mentioned her great admiration for flowers. While turning over the flowers and leaves, and examining

every little fibre she spoke enthusiastically of the beauties with which God had blessed us But said this feeling had passed away and she had lost all interest in the beauties of earth The reason she gave was that death was near at hand, and now her thoughts were ever turned upon the beauties of heaven and the glory she would soon enjoy with her blessed Lord

In a letter written by her son John in 1878, he says her Christian character and influence were not excelled by any woman of my acquaintance He does not know the exact time of her conversion She was charitable in giving and also in forgiving any who had either injured her or in any way deviated from the path of rectitude She spent much time in prayer for herself and her children. She would go to some quiet room in the house and pray for them by name until she had named the whole family and believed she had the promise of God that all would be saved

Her son Peter says he cannot tell when she was converted, but one thing he could say that when he was a little boy she prayed him asleep many nights

William says she was a Christian when a little girl.

I, Paul, add the following She was the mother of twelve children, eight sons and four daughters One son died when a child All the others grew up to man and womanhood during her life time Her Christian influence grew with them, so that at her death, or soon after all were Christians Her Christian work was not confined to her family but extended all through the

neighborhood where she lived, and I trust will continue to have its influence for ages to come. I was but a boy when at home with my dear mother, but can well remember many of her pious acts. Often have I heard her in the night, when she thought all were asleep, praying and pleading with God for hours in some quiet room for the conversion of her children and friends. When a boy eight or nine years old I went with her about five miles to see one of her daughters. She always rode on horseback and I had to ride behind, and as we went jogging along it took us about two hours. Her conversation during the whole journey was about her conversion and experiences in the Christian life. How happy she was and what joys she expected in meeting her Heavenly Father. She also gave me a description of heaven in her simple way of explaining it. The golden street she expected to walk upon. The robes and crown which would be placed upon her. The songs of praise she would hear and enjoy. Then exhorted and plead with me to give myself to the Saviour, be a child of God and meet her in heaven.

The last visit to my dear mother was on the first day of March, 1841. Shortly after our marriage, I, in company with my wife, drove over in a sleigh from Blairsville, Pa., to her home, near Pleasant Unity, a distance of twenty miles. We stopped at brother William's, and after warming ourselves and eating supper, we walked over to mother's house, it being but a short distance. On entering her chamber where she had been confined

for about ten days, she greeted us in a most loving and affectionate manner We spent the evening and the next morning with her When fearing the snow might leave us, we took our departure earlier than we expected, she gave us an affectionate farewell I had no idea when we left that it would be the last time I should ever see her But, alas, it was so. In a day or two she became very ill, and continued growing more feeble until the 12th, when she passed away We returned to Blairsville on our way over the mountains to Hollidaysburg, where we expected to make our home On the 15th I received a letter informing us of her death Many years have passed since this Christian mother went to her Heavenly home, but her influence and Christian example were so deeply impressed in the hearts and lives of all her children, that they have all been prominent in all Christian work, as the short history given of their lives will show

This letter was written to Peter, in Pittsburg

AT THE OLD HOME NEAR PLEASANT UNITY,
April 20th, 1836

TO MY SON PETER, HIS WIFE SUSAN, AND THEIR CHILDREN

I have received your kind present, which made me lie at the feet of Jesus, with humble gratitude O, may the lord fulfill his promise by giving you long life, and bless your soul

Are you seeking the lord, while he may be found? Make peace with your Redeemer while you are in the land of the living, as we cannot tell how soon the Lord may call us from time to eternity Turn to God and you will find peace in the blood of the Lamb

Call upon him until he prepares you for the Kingdom of Heaven Delay not your conversion Get an interest in the Lord as soon as possible by earnest prayer and faith

Remember him who has said many shall seek to enter in and not be able, let your fellowship be with the Father and his Son, Jesus Christ

Walk in the light as God is in the light, and the blood of Christ Jesus shall cleanse you from all sin O, my son, you must strive to enter in, agonize with all your power, there is nothing else that will support you in a dying hour Remember riches will not profit in the day of death, lay up your treasure in Heaven, and get your heart set on things above, and then the appearance of Christ will be joyful to you, because he will give you possession of Heaven Be often on your knees and earnest with the Lord, pray without ceasing, and then shall the Lord Jesus come and show us his glory, when the righteous shall shine as the sun in the Kingdom of their Father's house above to go out no more My dear son, your kind love made me think I could write I would be glad if you can read these few lines

My hand trembles so much I have to take both hands to shape a letter A poor speller, a weak head, a bad pen, a faint heart, a trembling hand, but still I do the best I can O that the Lord would renew my strength like the eagle, that I might learn more wisdom Lord Jesus, Amen

Yours in real affection

MOTHER B GRAFF

SCRAPS FROM OLD PAPERS OF MOTHER BARBARA GRAFF'S WRITING

Believers, what is Life? The end of it is but a living death, or dying life. It is full of grief for things past, full of labor for things

future The first part of our life is spent in folly; the middle part is overwhelmed with cares, and the latter part of it is burdened with cares, infirmities, and age, and what gain we by prolonging this life? Nothing but to suffer more evil, and should a Christian be willing to be rid of these grievances? Consider that dying is appointed as the only way to glory There is no way to enter the promised land but by crossing the Jordan of death, and rest.

O how I wander up and down, no one to pity me
I seem a stranger quite undone, a child of misery
None lend an ear to my complaint, nor mind my cries nor tears
None come to cheer me, though I faint nor burdens bear,
While others live in joy and mirth and feel no want nor woe,
I in this howling wilderness, still full of sorrow go
O, faithless soul to reason thus and murmur without end,
And has Christ expired upon the cross, and is he not thy friend?
The time is short, ye saints rejoice, the Lord will quickly come,
Soon shall you hear the bridegroom voice to call you to your home,
The time is short, the day is near that you shall dwell above,
And be forever happy then with Jesus whom you love

Now when death is at hand, let not my Saviour be afar off He who remembered the dying thief, and spoke comfortingly to him, now remember me

Take my soul and body's powers,
Take my memory, mind and will,
All my goods and all my hours,
All I know or speak or do,
Take my heart but make it new

Straight is the gate and narrow is the way which leadeth unto life, and few there be that find it

Let us ever remember that

> Thou, Oh, Lord, in tender love, dost all my burden bear ;
> Lift my heart to things above, and fix it ever there

The heart knoweth his own bitterness and a stranger doth not intermeddle with his joy

The heart is deceitful above all things, and desperately wicked Who can know it? I, the Lord

> Sometimes tempests blow a dreadful hurricane,
> And high the waters flow, and o'er my sides break in,
> But still my little ship outbraves
> The bursting winds and surging waves
> But when a heavenly breeze springs up and fills my sail,
> My vessel goes with ease before the pleasant gale,
> And runs as much an hour or more
> As in a month or two before

Rev 14 chap, 13 verse.—Blessd are the dead which die in the Lord From henceforth, yea saith the spirit, that they may rest from their labours, and their works do follow them

I.—HENRY GRAFF.

HENRY GRAFF, the eldest son of John and Barbara Graff, was born May 27th, 1794, and died September 9th, 1855. On September 19th, 1820, he married Elizabeth Lobingier, who was born April 3rd, 1800, and died July 19th, 1869. They were both buried at Pittsburg.

The birthplace of Henry was the old farm near Pleasant Unity, Westmoreland Co., Pa. From the time he was old enough until he was twenty years of age, he assisted his father in farming. After the death of his grandfather Henry Graff, in Germany, his father gave him a power of attorney and sent him there to settle and receive his share of the estate. He returned just before his father's death, which occurred December 31st, 1818. Before leaving Germany, he purchased a great many farming utensils, such as hay forks, shovels, spades, cutting knives, scythes, &c. As these articles were scarce and high here, they were sold at a handsome profit. Among the articles which came from grandfather's estate were tea and table spoons of silver, and a valuable old clock which played a number of tunes and struck quarters, half hours and hours. It was of the grandfather style, and was said to be an old clock when grandfather purchased it in 1700. It and the spoons still remain in the family.

In 1822 he commenced business in Pleasant Unity by keeping a country store, consisting of dry goods, groceries,

iron, fish, salt, &c His goods had to be hauled in wagons from Philadelphia and Baltimore As it took several weeks to transport them, the shipment was both tedious and expensive. He remained at Pleasant Unity about eleven years, and while there he taught his brothers Peter and Matthew the business His business prospered, and in order to give his brothers an interest in it he extended it and placed Peter in the small village of New Derry, about ten miles east of Greensburg After several years of success, Peter sold out and located at Blairsville, Indiana Co Henry then sold his Pleasant Unity store to John, his brother, and moved to Blairsville, where he and Peter formed a partnership and traded under the firm name of Henry and Peter Graff This was about the year 1833 They did a very extensive and profitable business and built a large grain house on the Conemaugh river in the town. A year or two afterwards Matthew was given an interest in the business

In 1836 Henry and Peter commenced the transportation of merchandise by railroad and canal, from Philadelphia and Baltimore, to Pittsburg and the west The line was called the Union Transportation Line Merchandise was carried by rail to Columbia, then by canal boat to Hollidaysburg, then by rail over the Alleghany mountains to Johnstown, then by canal to Pittsburg, 103 miles The canal and railroad were owned by the State of Pennsylvania.

Peter moved to Pittsburg and attended to receiving and forwarding the merchandise In a year or two the

forwarding business rapidly increased, and Henry also moved to Pittsburg, and he and Peter gave their whole attention to the business. A year afterwards he commenced the manufacturing of iron. He was a man of foresight, and was very successful in the iron business. He was a thoughtful and Christian man. One of the noble acts of his life in connection with his brother Peter, was stopping the running of canal boats on the Sabbath. The Philadelphia partners who were connected with the line—not having the same Christian views—were very much opposed to the project. The brothers, however insisted on a trial, so when the Sabbath came, boats were stopped (tied up as they called it), and man and beast rested on the Lord's day. The other transportation lines continued to run their boats as usual. The union line had posters put up at all public places in Philadelphia, Baltimore and the west, that they would stop on the Sabbath, and require a day longer to carry goods to Pittsburg. This went on for a few months, when the other lines were obliged to adopt the same policy, as the merchants preferred the line which rested on the Lord's day.

Henry continued in the transportation business for many years until the state sold out the canal and railroad in 1853. A Pittsburg paper said he was one of the leading citizens and the most active and successful commission merchant and iron manufacturer of the city. He was also successful in starting all his sons in business before his death, which occurred in 1855. He was for

many years a member of the Lutheran church, and one of the church pillars He was a liberal giver to his home church, and before his death, made a large contribution to the seminary at Gettysburg, Pa

CHILDREN OF HENRY AND ELIZABETH GRAFF

No 1—JOHN, born January 14th, 1822, unmarried

No 2—CHRISTOPHER, born October 2d, 1823

He married Arabella Blackmore, May 15th, 1858 She was born April 7th, 1839, died April 16th, 1866 Their children are

WM HENRY, born August 7th, 1859
JOHN C, born August 18th, 1861
ELIZABETH LOBENGIN, born January 24th, 1864

No 3—PRISCILLA SOPHIA, born March 31st, 1825

She was married to Paul Hugus, who was born Sept 29th, 1812, and died March 21st, 1879 Their children are.

HENRY GRAFF, born April 3d, 1847
EDWARD REED, born August 22d, 1848
ANNIE MARY, born February 17th, 1850

Edward married Lottie McClelland, who died Second marriage, Nancy Doak, no children

Anna Mary married Heberton C Negley, their children are

PAUL H, born
EDWARD H, born
JOHN C, born July 29th, 1855, died young.

No 4—William Graff, born December 27th, 1828

He married Isabella Coffin Their children are

Elizabeth, born
Anna Mary, born

No 5—Alexander Graff, born Nov 10th, 182[illegible], unmarried

No 6—Thos I Graff, born Oct 26th, 1832, died Apr 21st, 1890

He married Agnes C Dixon June 25th, 1863, who was born August 17th, 1847

Their children are eight in number as follows

John Dixon,	born	June 1st, 1864
Henry L,	"	" 18th, 1865
Bennett,	"	Mar 5th, 1867
Paul Hugus,	"	June 29th, 1869
Thomas Ewing,	"	Aug 21st, 1871
James Way,	"	May 25th, 1873
Matthew Addison,	"	Aug 23d, 1876
Agnes P,	"	June 11th, 1878

No 7—Matthew Graff born November 1st, 1834

He married Jane Addison, who was born 1839, and died Jan 1st, 1880 They had seven children

Henry Addison,	born	Dec 6th, 1863
Harriet Dugias,	"	Oct 1st, 1865
Mary K,	"	Dec 19th, 1867
Wm A Addison,	"	Jan 22d, 1871
Benj. Darlington	"	June 4th, 1877

Died December 22d, 1879.

RICHMAN MCCLURG, born June 4th, 1877
FRANCIS ERSKINE, " Mar 12th, 1879

Harriet married Robt R Singer April 30th, 1889 Children
JOHN ADDISON SINGER, born April 23d, 1890

No 8—ANNA MARY, born March 12th, 1837

She married John M Kirkpatrick, and her second husband Wm Pore No children

No 9—ELIZABETH, born April 29th, 1842 died Jan 19th, 1855

II.—MARY GRAFF.

Mary, the second child and eldest daughter of John and Barbara Graff, was born Sept 4th 1795, and died Dec. 4th, 1833 She was married to Jacob Lose, who was born June 8th, 1785, and died Dec 4th, 1820 She afterwards married John Lose, and lived near Pittsburg At her death she was buried at Homewood, Pa She was a devoted Christian, a member of the M E Church, and for many years conducted family worship regularly in her own house John, her eldest son says she prayed much and was very particular in training her children to become Christians and live a Godly life

CHILDREN OF JACOB AND MARY LOSE

No 1—John G, born July 10th 1814

He married Elizabeth L Smith, who was born April 11th, 1818 Their first child, Elizabeth born July 29th 1839, was married to Robert Waddle, March 2d, 1863 Their children are as follows

George Edward, born	Nov 29th, 1863		
Annie Mary "	Aug 22d, 1866		
Chas Franklin, "	Nov 27th, 1868		
Milton Howard, "	Aug 10th, 1871		
William B, born	Aug 22d, 1873,	died	Aug 12th, 1874
Lida Mary, "	Feb 2d, 1876,	"	Aug 5th, 1876

OLIVE BLANCHE, born Aug 12th, 1877
JESSIE BELL, " Aug 12th, 1880

ANNA, second daughter of John and Elizabeth Lose, was born Oct 5th, 1844 and married to George B Milholland Dec 18th, 1866 Their children are

JENNIE BOWER, born Sept 28th, 1867
JOHN LOSE, born April 15th, 1871, died March 20th, 1881
ANNA, born April 25th, 1873
GEORGE, " Feb 3rd, 1875, " Jan 11th, 1884
PORTER KERR, " " 26th, 1877, " June 16th, 1878
MARY ESTHER, born April 13th, 1879, died March 27th 1881
WILLIAM S., born Nov 28th, 1882
JAMES CONNELL, " " "
MARTHA LOGAN, " Oct 21st, 1884

WM HENRY, son of John and Elizabeth Lose, was born Oct 20th, 1849 He married Rhoda Mary Wells March 20th, 1875 Their children are

ANNIE ELIZA, born March 3rd, 1876
JENNIE ORLEAN, born Feb 8th, 1878, died Jan 6th, 1883
REX WELL, " " 24th, 1880 " " 2nd, "
MORRIS GRAFF, " Jan 16th, 1882, " Dec 23d, 1882

No 2—GEORGE, the second son of Jacob and Mary Lose, was born Oct 11th, 1816 He married Margaret Armel, Feb 19th, 1838 She was born May 1st, 1822, and died April 2nd, 1845 They had three children.

(1) SARAH E., was born March 16th, 1840. She married I. J Hammer, Nov 10th, 1858 Their children are Margaret, Lydia, all married and living in Missouri

(2) ARMEL, born July 1st, 1842, died Aug 11th, 1842

(3) CHRISTOPHER G, born March 21st, 1845, and died in the army Dec 12th, 1864

GEORGE LOSE was married a second time, Jan 2nd, 1848, to Margaret Elder, who was born Sep 22nd, 1830

Their children were (1) Charles R, born Nov 12th, 1849 He married Libbie S Touch, Sep 22nd, 1875 To them were born four children

GEORGE L,	born	Sep 18th,	1876
SALLIE E,	"	July	1878
WILLIAM L,	"	Jan 29th,	1882
MARGARET E,	"	Aug	1885

(2) JACOB ELDER, born Nov 25th, 1851. He married Sadie C. Graham June 28th, 1881 They have two children

EMMA V,	born	April 17th,	1882
ROBERT G	"	Oct. 15th,	1883

(3) MARY ELDER, born Sep 11th, 1854, was married to J. Osborne, Dec 25th, 1885 They have two children

MARGARET LOSE,	born	Sept 21st,	1884
ROBERT MILTON,	"	Oct 18th,	1886

(4) VIOLET, born Jan 4th, 1859

(5) EMMA I born May 31st, 1860, was married to P R Douglas, March 17th, 1886

(6) GEORGE, JR, born May 6th, 1863

(7) ANNA C, born June 10th, 1872

No 3—JACOB LOSE, born May 17th, 1818, died 1873, at Mobile.

(3) VIRGINIA was born July 11th, 1845, died Sept 2nd, 1848

(4) EMMA L, was born Oct 3rd, 1848 She was married Aug 12th 1869, to Rufus McClain, who was born March 20th, 1842 Children

JOHN REED born June 27th 1870 died , 1880

ED C, born Nov 27th, 1882

Mr McClain was a soldier during the civil war, and is now a farmer living in Kansas

(5) JOSEPH DEMPSEY was born March 1st, 1851 He married Nevada A Chandler, April 11th, 1875 She was born Dec 4th, 1854 Their children are

JOSEPH CLYDE, born June 30th, 1876
JESSE E, " Aug 26th, 1877
LILLY C, " Nov 3rd, 1878
ALBERT E, " Mar 29th, 1880
FORD D, born Sep 9th, 1881, died Nov 1881

Mr Reed is a merchant in Belle Plain, Kansas

(6) JOHN LOCKE, born April 3rd, 1854, died Nov 1854

(7) SARAH KATE, born Nov 27th, 1855, died Sept 1st, 1859

(8) WM LEVI, born Jan 11th, 1859, is now living in Belle Plain, Kansas

(9) SEGEL CURTIS, born March 12th, 1862 He married Kate E Cully, Oct 8th, 1882

(10) INFANT SON, born and died June 25th, 1865

No 5—LEVI LOSE was born Feb 24th, 1821

He married Susan Fisher March 4th, 1842 She was born June 24th, 1822, and died Nov 1st 1862 Their children and grandchildren are as follows

(1) WESLEY F, born April 11th, 1841 On Dec 3rd, 1865, he married Rachel Fugit, who was born Sept 26th, 1837 They had four children

JENNIE, born Dec 19th, 1866
CLARA, " Sept 4th, 1868
MURRY D " Oct 20th 1872
ROBERT LEVI, " Nov 11th, 1878

(2) SARAH ANN, born Jan 31st, 1847 On Jan 14th 1863, she was married to John Johnston, who was born Dec 25th, 1842 Children

SUSAN, born Nov 28th, 1863
JANE, " Sept, 22nd, 1867
MARY A, born Feb 15th, 1870, died March 1st, 1873
GEORGE " Sept 10th, 1873, " Oct 18th, 1874
EMMA E, born Jan 10th, 1874
FRANKIE L, " Sept 7th 1875
JAMES L, " Apr. 7th, 1878

(3) EMMA E, born Aug 19th, 1849 On Nov 30th 1865, she was married to Joseph Bunn, who was born Aug 23rd 1846 Children

EMMA R, born Jan 14th, 1867 died Jan 19th, 1874
INFANT SON, " Feb 19th, 1869, " Feb 19th 1869
WILLIAM, born Feb 13th, 1870

MARY ANN, born April 28th, 1872, died Oct 22nd, 1874
INFANT SON, " Mar 24th, 1874, " Mar 24th, 1874
SILAS NYE, " July 13th, 1875, " Sept 8th, 1875
EDWARD, born Dec 30th, 1876
JOSEPH F, born Sept 10th, 1878, died Mar 2nd, 1881
CHARLES H, born Jan 3rd, 1881, died Jan 3rd, 1881
BERTIL O born Jan 31st, 1882
RICHARD " Feb 15th, 1884
Jesse O " Mar 5th, 1886
ADOLPHUS, born Aug 31st, 1861, remains single

(4) On Jan 28th, 1863, Levi Lose married as his second wife, Sarah Fugit, who was born June 25th, 1828 Children

(5) RACHEL C, born Jan 20th, 1864 She was married to Frederick Hawk, Nov 27th, 1880 Their child Lillie was born Jan 18th, 1881 Mrs Hawk was again married to Hansford W Eggleston, Sept 27th, 1885 Mr Eggleston was born March, 18th, 1859 Their children were

JESSIE AND BESSIE, born July 16th, 1886

(6) WM SHERMAN, born Feb. 3rd, 1865, remains single

(7) ELLA E, born May, 28th 1868, remains single

III.—SARAH GRAFF.

SARAH GRAFF, the third child and second daughter of John and Barbara Graff, was born May 3d, 1797, died Sept. 16th, 1850 She married Daniel Barnes Dec 19th, 1820. He died in Aug 1858 They are both buried at Johnstown, Pa

They were members of the M E Church She was a devoted Christian woman and spent much of her time in Christian work During the season for camp meetings they were always among the first to pitch their tents and be ready for work Many Christian people enjoyed a good meal at their table

Children and grandchildren as follows:

No 1—MARGARET GRAFF, born Apr 14th, 1823, died, 1845

No 2—JOHN W GRAFF, born Nov 7th, 1824

He was married Dec 30th, 1847 to Kezia Cooper, who was born Feb 17th, 1830 Children

(1) WILBUR A, born Nov 14th, 1848 married Helan Gayland Feb 14th, 1881 Their child Elizabeth was born March, 1882

(2) SARAH J, born Sept 21st, 1850, married Wm F Ritchie April 14th, 1870 Their two children are Hattie J., born May 1871, and Addison C, born Sep 1875, died Jan 16th, 1884

(3) ALMIRA C, born July 8th 1852, married David McCullough June 29th, 1873 Six Children

WM E.,	born	April, 1874
JOHN H.,	"	July, 1876
JOSEPH O	"	April, 1879
KEZIA M	"	July, 1881
ANNIE M.,	"	Mar., 1883
JESSIE F.,	"	May, 1885

(4) LOVENIA A, born Aug 30th, 1854, married James W Thompson Oct 16th, 1877 One child, Walter W, was born July 1878

(5) HENRY B, born Sep 11th, 1856 Married Sadie E Jameson Dec 22d, 1880. Three children

ROBERT W,	born April, 1882;	died June, 1882
JESSIE C,	" June, 1883,	" Jan 1884
ORA C,	" Feb 1885	

(6) JAMES C, born Sep 11th, 1856, (twin brother of Henry B) married Mattie E Jameson Dec 22d, 1880 Two children

MAUD K,	born July, 1882
FRANCIS E,	" Mar 1885

(7) SAMUEL W, born Aug 20th, 1860 Married Mary E. Dent, Sept 17th, 1885

(8) JOSEPH G, born Oct 10th 1862

(9) REBECCA M, " Dec, 23d, 1865

(10) AMANDA M," Mar 24th, 1868

No 3—ELIZABETH BARNES, born Feb 6th, 1827, died Jan 20th, 1868 Married Joseph P Graham, born Nov 9th, 1848

Nine children

(1) DAN'L H, born Nov 13th, 1849, died Oct 27th, 1855

(8) FORD " Jan 9th, 1871

(9) LUCIUS and ELLA, born Dec 13th, 1873

(10) Child, born 1855, died in infancy

No 5—LUCY BARNES, born Oct 31st, 1831
Lucy married Jacob Trefts, July 2d 1851 nine children

(1) DANIEL, born Aug 5th, 1852, died 1853

(2) ADAM, born Feb 7th, 1854
Adam married Clara Hess, Dec 23rd, 1879, one child
WALTER, born Feb 11th, 1881

(3) CHARLES, born Aug 29th, 1856
Charles married Augusta Elfers, Jan 1st, 1883
EDGAR, J., born April 1st, 1885

(4) GEO born Jan 30th, 1859, died 1860

(5) EDWARD, born May 19th, 1861

(6) MARY, born Oct 18th, 1864
Mary married Henry Hans June 16th 1885

(7) FRANK, born Sept 5th, 1856, died Sept 22d, 1880.

(8) ANNIE, born Sept 18th, 1868

(9) RALPH, born July 30th 1871

No 6—BARBARA, born Jan 13th, 1834

No 7.—ALEX, born 1838, drowned April, 1853

No 8—WM GRAFF, died in infancy

No 9.—PAUL GRAFF, " "

IV.—WILLIAM GRAFF

William Graff, the second son of John and Barbara Graff, was born Oct 1st, 1798, died Nov., 1882 He married Sarah Reed, who was born March 8th, 1804 and died Aug 24th, 1881 Both buried at Pleasant Unity, Westmoreland county, Pa. They had no children

He was one of the brothers, who, after his father's death, continued with his mother on the farm, doing the principle farming, after his marriage which occurred February 26th, 1826. He then took charge of the Poorman farm about one-half mile south of Pleasant Unity After his mother's death he purchased it, and lived on it until his death

Wm. Graff was a devoted Christian and an active member of the M E Church for fifty-four years His wife was converted and joined the church first She insisted on her husband seeking an interest in Christ, but he said he could not pray She told him to get down on his knees and she would pray for him They both knelt down, she prayed and he cried unto the Lord until his cries were heard He was a man of great energy of character, and this appeared in his Christian life He prayed much both at home and with his brethren Once when returning home from a visit to his brother's, and waiting at the R R Station, he went into the room and found a number of men playing cards He stood and looked at them a moment and then said. "Men, do you

know the Lord sees you." and then turned away At another time a friend riding with him in the country, said Bro Graff "we will stop here a few minutes" At this he called for a Bible read a long chapter and prayed a long prayer He stopped and prayed twice at least and they did not get home until late at night He paid a visit to his minister and after the usual greeting and inquiry about church matters he said "Brother, give me a Bible and I will read a chapter and pray before leaving" These may be called eccentricities, but they indicate the earnestness of his religious life

The following obituary was published after his death

OBITUARY

The death of Wm Graff on Saturday, Nov 18, 1882, at his home near Pleasant Unity, removes the last of a very remarkable family from among the citizens of this county Wm Graff was the second born of seven sons and four daughters, all of whom lived to be married

John Graff, the father, owned and lived on the farm on which Mr Blank now resides He also owned the farm on which Wm lived and died The father died Dec 31, 1818, aged 57 years

Barbara, the mother, died March 12, 1841, aged 66 years She is still remembered in this community as a woman of extraordinary piety Many remember to have heard her voice in prayer, in the night, as they passed her house Her habit was to take her children in order and by name present their case to God, wrestling with Him for each until she felt she had prevailed and they would be saved

No wonder that a family on whose childhood descended the

baptism of such prayers from such a mother, should be prominent among men and useful in the church

Henry Graff, deceased, began business as a merchant, in Pleasant Unity, but removed to Pittsburg, where he was a prominent "forwarding merchant" His family are among the leading business men of that city to-day

John Graff also began as a merchant in our town, but removed to Blairsville, where he still lives a hale old man, never sick an hour in his life, a patriarch in the town and one of the fathers of the M E Church His sons are among the solid men of that community

Peter Graff is a very successful business man of Armstrong county, Pa and an officer in the Lutheran Church His sons bid fair even to surpass their father as wealth getters

Jacob Graff, at one time a hatter in this town, again a mill owner near Derry, is now a mill owner in Illinois, and a member of the M E Church

Matthew Graff is a merchant near Alliance, Ohio, and an elder in the Presbyterian Church

Paul Graff, the well known wholesale shoe dealer of Philadelphia, is also an elder of the Presbyterian Church Of the daughters, Mrs Lose and Mrs Barnes have been dead for years, but their offspring may be found somewhere near Johnstown, Pa and many in different parts of the west Mrs Colleasure, widow of an elder of the Presbyterian Church, and Mrs Armstrong are living in Illinois

Wm Graff was born October 10th 1798, died November 18th 1882, and was married to Sarah R Read, February 26th, 1826, by Rev N P Hacke She died August 24th, 1881 Though they were never blessed with children of their own during their life together, several found a home with them and a place in their

hearts They lived a quiet, happy life together for 55½ years They died a little more than a year apart, rejoicing in the Christian's hope

Bro Graff was a zealous member of the M E Church, of Pleasant Unity, for 54 years His religious convictions were very positive, and he was very free to express them He was in the habit of visiting his neighbors and praying with their families Many who in health thought him fanatical, were glad to have him sing and pray with them when sick or dying

Brother Graff was kindly nursed by Miss Mary Wyand who has been in the family for over ten years, and his nephew, Mr Reed, of Kansas

An interesting and impressive funeral service, conducted by Rev McCurdy, his pastor, assisted by Rev Ferier, of the Reformed church was held in the M E church, Tuesday Nov 21st, at 11 a m, before a very large congregation of the friends and neighbors

While the casket was being placed before the altar, a choir of young girls led by E G Walter, sang softly "Asleep in Jesus" The pastor then read the ritual and Rev Ferier offered prayer The congregation sang, "We Know by Faith We Know" After reading Second Corinthians 5th, 1-7, Rev McCurdy spoke for thirty minutes of the religious convictions and life of the departed The congregation then sang a hymn The remains were then taken to the old Bethel church yard, by the side of his wife

V.—JOHN GRAFF.

JOHN GRAFF, the third son of John and Barbara Graff, was born August 3rd, 1800, near Pleasant Unity, Westmoreland Co., Pa. Beginning life almost with the beginning of our Republic, he drank in its early spirit of enterprise, patriotism and love of liberty. His entire life became a picture of "strength and beauty." He inherited a strong physical constitution, which was early developed by the work and fare of farm life. He maintained his great strength until the natural decay of old age, and remained until death, as erect in form as he had been upright in character. With him the wants of his physical nature were always an interesting study. He never assumed to have the knowledge of a doctor, but such was his understanding of the human system, and the confidence of others in his judgment in cases of sickness, that, whenever any of his grandchildren were taken sick, the first thing to do was to "send for Grandfather."

Little can be said of his school life. He attended the subscription school of his day, and for two months in each of the winters, when he was sixteen and seventeen years old, he attended the Greensburg Academy. Limited though his time for study was, he yet laid a good foundation for the future, and became thoroughly imbued with a desire to learn. This desire never left him, but became one of the striking characteristics of his life. Whatever of his success is to be attributed to his own persistent

effort, the right direction of that effort is largely due to the strong life and character of his mother Strong in body, and just as strong in spirit, walking daily in the strength of the Lord.

John remained on the farm until 1833, his father having died Dec 31st, 1818 While on the farm at the age of twenty-four, he married Lucy Sophia Hacke, of Baltimore She was but a girl, and knew literally nothing about farm life, but she became a true helpmate to him. She died March 4th, 1877, at the age of seventy-one

During his stay on the farm, an incident occurred which clearly illustrates one of the traits of his character

A distillery was attached to the farm, as was common in those days He observed that men became intoxicated by the use of the liquor, and believing it was wrong, decided that it should not be manufactured there any longer

Ever after he was a staunch friend of the temperance cause, holding in that early day temperance principles that were fifty years ahead of his times

On quitting the farm, he entered the mercantile business in Pleasant Unity Here he stayed for three years, until 1837, when he moved to Blairsville, Pa, and purchased a half-interest in the warehouse built by his brothers Henry and Peter In 1847 he assumed control of the entire business, and continued in it until his death. The business rapidly increased until nearly all the produce of Indiana and Westmoreland Counties passed through his hands Two other houses were put up on the banks of the old canal Business relations brought

him into contact with men far and near He won the respect and confidence of all. It was in this hand to hand contact with men that he impressed upon them his own strong convictions on all questions of public interest.

His method of impressing the truth was peculiar. His object was, not to make men angry, but to bring them to his way of thinking He could reason, and reason well, but he preferred, like Abraham Lincoln, to let the light into men's minds by some laughable anecdote which served as an illustration

His habit was to earnestly seek for the right in any disputed question. When found, he followed it wherever it led, no matter what the opposition might be This habit of searching for the truth and adopting it with all his heart, generally led him to advanced grounds on all great questions, and hence ahead of his age This made him a leader of opinion, and also a leader of men

In his early manhood, he very materially aided in securing the system of free schools in the township where he lived

More than anywhere else his strong convictions and the strong stand which he made for them was shown in his attitude toward the slavery question In the agitation of that great cause, it soon became a question among the churches whether a man could be a consistent Christian, and at the same time a supporter of a political party which did not favor the abolition of the slaves Although he granted men full liberty of opinion, yet his own political attitude was such as to be a rebuke to many who had

not the courage to take the stand which he took. At first he was a member with others of the Whigs, but failing to see any relief coming from that source, he joined The Liberty Party. By this party he was made a candidate for the legislature. This brought him into more prominence, and the opposition to his convictions soon became opposition to himself. The bitter feeling even entered into the church of which he was a member, but in the midst of all opposition, he stood firmly and kindly. The time was not yet ripe for the breaking of old party ties, and he was defeated at the election. He afterwards became a member of the Republican Party, and through this party saw his desires for the slave fulfilled.

His efforts to help fugitive slaves to Canada would be an interesting chapter in his life, could we but know all that he did. Certainly he was a very active agent of the "underground railway," of that day. When the fugitive slave laws were passed, he was asked by a pro-slavery man if he would catch a runaway slave if ordered to do so. "Of course I would," and after the expression of surprise on the part of the pro-slavery man, he added, "but I would soon whisper in the slave's ear, that, if he would try he could easily break away from me."

It was one of the beautiful traits of his character from his boyhood up, that he always took the part of the weak and the oppressed.

His religious life and experience are interesting. He could not well help having a religious mind on account of the influence of his mother's life. He was early taught

in the word of God, and the doctrines of the Reformed church On coming to Blairsville, he joined the Methodist Episcopal Church, toward which he had always leaned, and was made by the church a classleader. For a number of years he labored in this position, honestly and sincerely, it is true, but, as he afterwards confessed, having the "form" without the "power of godliness" Several things greatly annoyed him in his class-meetings When members became happy, some of them would express their religious joy in harsh, unpleasant tones, while others would rejoice aloud Both of these, he thought, were out of place in a solemn religious service, but his good sense prevented him from offending any by repressing these expressions of feeling. Finally, during a season of revival, he was convinced by the Holy Spirit that there was a power in religion which he had never experienced So deeply was he convicted that he could not sleep About three o'clock one morning, he rose from his bed, and started for the kitchen that he might pray alone The prayer in his heart was, "Lord if there is power of which I know nothing, reveal it to me" The Lord answered his prayer, and as he was passing the dining room table, the power of God so fell upon him as to literally prostrate him. And ever after, his religion was one of "power" Consistent with his own experience, he always sought to lead men directly to God The salvation of men was his chief concern He was regular and punctual at all the church services, not even neglecting the Wednesday evening prayer meeting He was a liberal and cheerful

giver to the church to every good cause The worthy poor were never turned away empty He stood at his post, as class-leader in the church, until death released him He was always a great help in revival meetings, and was frequently called to assist in meetings in surrounding churches It was while attending such a meeting at the Methodist Church at Homer, between Blairsville and Indiana, that he took the cold that resulted in his death The theme of his talk that night was Naaman, the Leper, his favorite subject when addressing sinners He dwelt on this because it so exactly described the humiliation of his own proud spirit, before he fully knew the *saving power* of God

Death had no "terror" and no "sting" for him About the middle of January, 1885, he showed signs of rapid failure. He lingered several weeks, until the 31st of the month, when he "crossed over," and was at rest During his sickness his mind was clear—in fact it was to the very end He suffered intensely at the last, but his soul was exceedingly happy He accepted all as from his Lord and recognized in his sufferings his last earthly trial When suffering most, he quoted the sentiment of that beautiful hymn ·

"When through fiery trials thy pathway shall lie
"My grace, all-sufficient shall be thy supply,
"The flame shall not hurt thee, I only design
"Thy dross to consume, and thy gold to refine."

The "grace" was "all-sufficient," for in spite of the pain, his soul became exultingly happy, and he praised God with a loud voice He exhorted all who visited him, and all his children to be faithful unto God till death.

An incident occurred a few days before his death, showing the loving Christian character of the man An Irish woman (Catholic), to whom he had often given advice, and assisted her to invest her little earnings, as soon as she heard he was sick, called to see him On entering the room next to his sick chamber, she was met by one of his sons, who said his father was too ill and could not be seen She expressed great sorrow. On his return to his father's chamber, he asked who it was that wished to see him His son replied, Aunt Kettee Burns His father said at once, bring her in After the usual greeting, she expressed great sympathy for him in his sufferings He then repeated the beautiful hymn, "Jesus lover of my soul, &c" After leaving his room, she said, if there ever was a Christian, Mr Graff was one

He knew he was dying, but repeatedly quoted his favorite hymn. "By death I shall escape from death, and life-eternal gain."

His mind at the last was fixed upon the Master whom he had served so faithfully and lovingly, and his last words were, "Lord! Lord!"

The following poem was written by one who saw him die and heard his death-bed utterances These utterances are indicated by quotation marks The poem is entitled

THE CROSSING

By the brink of the mystic river,
Flowing noiselessly along,
As an eager pilgrim waited
(For his feet had lingered long,)
To his listening ear was wafted,
A strain of the new, new song

"Glory to Him that hath loved us!"
Blessing was borne on the strain
Forgot were his hours of sorrow,
And the weary weight of pain,
For the Heavenly music thrilled him,
And his soul was glad again

Did a ray of glory tremble
From the Father's throne above
On the joyful lips that murmured,
As he saw his fears removed?
"To think He should touch me, *even me*,
With the finger of His love"

Still silently flowed the river,
So darksome and deep and wide
Vainly he looked for a crossing
Over the hurrying tide,
But his faith cried all victorious,
"And the waters He'll divide."

As he viewed with longing vision,
The loved on the other side,
Faint came the tremulous whisper,
"And the waters he'll divide"
Then his Lord came closer, closer,
And he leaned upon his guide

Gently the waters divided,
For his Lord passed through before,
And a hand unseen upheld him,
Till he gained the further shore
Aye the love that stooped to touch him,
Now enfolds him evermore

The funeral services were held in the Methodist church, and, although the church is a large one, there were more people outside who could not get into the church, than there were inside It seemed as though the entire neighborhood was present, there being many also from a distance. The services were in charge of Rev J W. Miles, with all the ministers of the town assisting Addresses were made by Drs. Hill and Davis, of the Presbyterian church, who had both been his life-long friends His grave was made by the side of his wife's grave in the Blairsville cemetery

"Blessed are the dead who die in the Lord
"Their trials are past, their work is done,
"And they are fully blest
"They fought the fight, the victory won,
"And entered into rest"

The following is a list of the posterity of John and Lucy Graff.

The children of John Graff were:

(1) Susanna born June 25th, 1825, died July 10th, 1825

(2) Henry, " Sept 9th, 1826

(3) Caroline, " Dec 10th, 1828, died May 16th, 1882

(4) Alexander, born July 2d, 1831

(5) Jacob, born Sept 23rd, 1834

(6) Nicholas, born Oct 1836, died 1839

(7) Paul, born July 4th, 1838

(8) James, " Jan 1841 died May 11th, 1860

(9) Edward, born Feb 12th 1843 died March 1845

(10) Charles H., born Feb. 6th, 1846

(11) Mary, born Jan 10th, 1850, died March 16th, 1850

Marriages of Above and Children

No. 2—Henry married Margaret Wilkenson Oct 30th, 1848

George K., born Sept 18th, 1849 died Oct 10th, 1851

Lucy L., born Apr 15th, 1851.

Mary K., " Oct 30th, 1852

John E., born June 16th, 1854, died May 6th, 1856

Charles L., born Feb 12th, 1856

Mary L., " Oct 2d, 1857

James G., born March 14th, 1860.

Caroline A., born July 28th 1863 died Nov 14th 1864

Sumner, born Sept 6th 1865

Gertrude M. " Oct 28th, 1867

Albert P. born Oct 28th 1873 died Dec 8th 1873

No 3—CAROLINE married Alexander Shields May 2d, 1850 The former died May 16th, 1882 and the latter Jan, 1863 Their children were

LUCY S, born May 7th 1852, died April 10th, 1887

(1) Lucy married Alfred Porter Kirtland Oct 7th, 1876, who was born May 24th, 1844 Children's births and names are

RUTH C, born Jan 20th, 1880
JOHN SHIELDS," " 3rd, 1880

(2) JOHN G, born Jan 10th, 1854

John married Esther Kendall Oct 9th, 1884, in Grand Rapids, Mich Now living at Colorado Springs, Col One child

GEORGE KENDALL SHIELDS, born Jan 27th, 1887

(3) BELLA, born March 6th, 1855, died March 18th, 1862

(4) MARY, " " 1st, 1857

(5) ALEXANDER D, born Dec, 16th, 1858

(6) CAROLINE, born April 21st, 1860

Caroline married Sept 24th, to Edwin R Morse born July 3rd, 1857 Children's names and births

EDWIN A, born Sept 30th, 1888
LUCILLE, " Dec 3rd, 1889

No 4—ALEXANDER GRAFF married Mary Wilkenson Feb 27th, 1856 Their children were

(1) JOHN A, born Jan 27th, 1859
(2) DENISON W born Oct 10th, 1859, died March 14th, 1861.
(3) EDGAR I, " Jan 10th 1862
(4) HERBERT P " Sept 21st 1864
(5) LUELLA, " Dec 29th, 1866

(6) Annie R., " April 1st, 1869
(7) James F., " Sept, 23rd 1871
(8) Mary W., " Jan 24th, 1874.
(9) Alfred H " March 21st, 1877

No 5—Jacob Graff married Sallie E R Davis, Aug 11th, 1864 There children are

(1) Annie Parkhill, born Feb 14th, 1871, adopted
(2) William F, born Aug 15th, 1874

No 7—Paul Graff married Elizabeth Mowry, Oct 23rd, 1860 Their children were

(1) George R, born Oct 2d, 1861
(2) Frank M, " Dec 1st 1865
(3) Annie, " Dec 7th, 1867, died Dec 9th 1867
(4) Wilbur P., " Dec 18th, 1868
(5) Laura M " July 7th, 1871
(6) Walter R., " Sept, 18th, 1874

No 10—Charles H Graff married Maggie Laughry Sept 15th, 1868 Their children were

(1) Allison, born Oct 11th, 1869, died Aug 12th, 1870
(2) Robert C, born Jan 18th, 1871
(3) Ramond, born March 30th, 1874

Obituary and Other Notices of John Graff from the Newspaper, "The Enterprise," Blairsville, Pa

Mr John Graff, Sr, after an illness of several weeks, died at his home, in this place, on Saturday Never since we have been in Blairsville has there been a death which caused such universal

regret among all classes Mr Graff having been engaged in active business here for nearly fifty years, had made the acquaintance of almost every person in this and Westmoreland counties He was a truly Christian gentleman, and his many deeds of kindness had gained him the respect of every one who knew him In business, politics, and in fact everything in which he engaged he was strictly honorable His opinions very often conflicted with those of his associates, and his place of business was the scene of many warm discussions When any new questions came before the public, he would make a careful study of it before forming an opinion, and when his mind was made up on the side which he thought was right—and he was seldom in the wrong—he was not afraid to speak his convictions He opposed slavery with his whole heart when few men had the courage to speak against it

His funeral services were held in the M E church, on Monday afternoon The large audience room was completely packed with people, and many went away unable even to find standing room A special train brought a number of persons from Indiana At 2 P M the corpse was carried into the church, followed by a large number of relatives After the introductory exercises, Rev Miles read the following brief sketch of Mr Graff's life

"John Graff, Sr, was born in Westmoreland Co, Pa, near Pleasant Unity, Aug 3rd, 1800, and died at his home in Blairsville, Jan 31st, 1885 His early educational advantages were limited, but were so diligently improved as to give to him a safe and broad foundation for intellectual pursuits He was throughout life, a careful student of men and literature He was married in 1824, to Lucy S Hacke Mrs Graff died in 1877, eight years ago Of the eleven children that were born to them, five sons are living, and are well known in this community He moved to Blairsville in 1837, and became one of the active business men of the place He had formerly been a member of the German

Reformed Church After his removal to Blairsville, he connected himself with the Methodist Episcopal Church, and continued a member the remainder of his life, with the exception of a few years that he was connected with the Wesleyan Methodist Church He was honored by the church with many positions of trust, and proved himself an efficient officer At the time of his death he was a class-leader He had been reared under decidedly religious influences, and inherited from his parents a clear sense of justice and a strong love of human rights Hence he was in the best and and broadest sense, the friend of humanity, the law of kindness was in his tongue and in his heart His absorbing theme and supreme delight was the salvation of men He was in advance of his day on all questions of moral reform, and having the courage of his convictions, he stood in the forefront of the battle of God and humanity In his death, his family, this church, the entire community, have sustained a great loss, but he has realized the blessedness and victory of one of his familiar quotations

'By death I shall escape from death,
And life eternal gain ' "

Rev Geo Hill, D D, of the Presbyterian church, and Rev Jas Davis, both warm friends of the deceased, made brief but touching addresses in evidence of his true Christian character Rev Miles then recounted some of the scenes of his last illness, showing that as the end drew near, Mr Graff had no fears for the future Another useful life is ended, and although it is hard for friends to part with him, they have the consolation of knowing that he has gone to a world where trouble never comes His life had been spent in the service of his Master, and he has been taken to his reward During his illness he talked of the goodness of God, and at times, in spite of his intense suffering, he would become extremely happy His last words were, "Lord Lord!"

OBITUARY NOTICES FROM OTHER PAPERS

HON. JOHN GRAFF, of Blairsville, after a brief illness, died at his residence in this town, on Saturday last, Jan. 31st. He was born in Westmoreland Co., near Pleasant Unity, Aug. 3rd, 1800. He was married in 1824, to Miss Lucy Hacke, who bore him eleven children, five of whom survive, to wit: Henry, Alexander, Paul, Jacob and Charles.

At an early day he located in Blairsville, and after the opening of the Pennsylvania Canal, erected a warehouse on the bank of the river, and through that house passed nearly all the produce of the county. In that connection he had business relations with a great many persons, and his acquaintanceship extended to the northern limits of our county. He was highly esteemed by all as an honest, upright man, and he had the most implicit confidence of all who dealt with him. His early education was not great, yet he acquired an extensive knowledge of men and measures. He was a strong advocate of equal rights, and an active anti-slavery man, and on more than one occasion assisted the closely pursued slave to escape to a land of freedom. He was a man of strong religious proclivities, and his whole life was an exemplification of the beauties of Christianity. He was, in the broadest sense, a friend of humanity, and never turned an unwilling ear to the cry of distress, from whatever quarter it came. In his business relations with his fellow-men he was correct, and his word was as good as his bond. In the financial affairs of his church, he was always a liberal and cheerful giver, and out of his abundance, he made many hearts glad by his private charities. In stature and appearance he was a noble looking man, and bore the impress upon his face of the kindness and nobility which permeated his whole character and life. The funeral services took place in the M. E. Church, on Monday afternoon last, and were attended by almost the entire populace of this place, many being

unable to gain admission The services were conducted by the ministers of the town, Dr. Hill, of the Presbyterian Church, delivering the sermon The services were very impressive and the strict attention and many tearful eyes in the audience gave strong evidence of the esteem in which he was held by his fellow-citizens who turned out in such large numbers to pay a last sad tribute to one they had learned to love, and to whom so many of them had looked up to for advice in spiritual matters His death was cheerful and his last words gave evidence that he knew that a crown of glory awaited him in the mansions of the Master he had so faithfully served His last days were made pleasant by the faithful and untiring efforts of his children to care for his every want and comfort In the death of John Graff the people of Blairsville have lost one of their best citizens, and the church a faithful worker But his example will live long after his remains shall have returned to the dust from which they came, and his noble life will be a hand-board to those who desire to honorably and acceptably serve the Master A special train left this place at 1 P M, bearing quite a number of our people who desired to be present at the funeral obsequies

DEATH has again been among us, and claimed as its victim a father in Israel Mr John Graff, Sr, died at his residence on Liberty street, on last Saturday morning, in the 85th year of his age His funeral services were held at the M E Church on Monday afternoon, and was largely attended In the immense crowd which assembled to pay the last tribute of respect to the departed, all denominational distinctions were forgotten in the great sorrow that had fallen upon the community in the loss of one of its oldest and most respected citizens Catholics and Protestants of all denominations alike paid their tribute to the honored dead, and mourned the loss they sustained in the death of this

venerable citizen Rev George Hill Rev James Davis, and the pastor, J M Miles, spoke in the highest terms of the Christian character of the deceased, and of his many noble and generous qualities which were characteristic of him throughout his entire life Mr Graff was born in August, 1800, in Westmoreland county, near Unity In 1837 he removed to this place and engaged in business Since that time to the time of his death he has been a resident of this place, and has been eminently successful in his business In the death of Mr Graff the community sustains a severe loss, while the church is bereft of one of its most useful and earnest members. The friends of the deceased have the sympathy of the entire community in their sad bereavement

DEATH OF MR JOHN GRAFF, SR

SATURDAY last, the 31st ult, saw the close of a life of usefulness and activity when the venerable John Graff, Sr, of Blairsville, passed beyond the realms of time to eternity, with a full consciousness and hope of a blessed immortality He was born August 3, 1800, near Pleasant Unity, Westmoreland Co, was married to Miss Lucy S Hacke in 1824, and removed to Blairsville in 1837, where he has been since largely engaged in business

He was a man of splendid physique, standing over six feet in height, and in his prime was a powerful man Not only a powerful man physically but a man of strong mind and firm convictions, as all who were acquainted with him well know

The funeral services took place on Monday afternoon, the remains being removed to the audience hall of the M E Church, which was filled to its utmost capacity The services were opened by a voluntary by the choir, after which a lesson from the Scriptures was read by Rev J A ——ter, and the beautiful hymn "Jesus Lover of my Soul," given out by Rev Stevens, and

sung Rev Miles, the pastor of the church, then read a brief memorial of the life of the deceased, and then introduced Dr Hill, of the Presbyterean Church, as the first speaker Dr Hill delivered a beautiful and eloquent tribute to his old friend, whom he had known for over forty-three years, and was followed by Rev Davis and Rev J W Miles, the pastor of the church The services were closed by prayer by Rev Thomas, of the U P Church, after which the immense audience passed around the bier of their old friend and neighbor to take a last look at the remains of one, who although silent in death, had been in life a power, and who left a bright example to his family and friends and the entire community His remains were then interred in the Blairsville cemetery followed by a large concourse of people

The business houses and railroad shops were closed and business suspended, and the general regret of all the citizens but feebly expressed the grief and sorrow of the community at the loss of one of their first citizens

The deceased has five sons living—Henry, Alexander Paul, Jacob and Charles—all active and energetic business men, and if we are correctly informed, three of his brothers, younger in years, are still living—the family connections being one of the largest in this county

JOHN GRAFF'S DEATH—GREENSBURG PAPER

FEW men in Western Pennsylvania were better known among business men than John Graff of Blairsville On last Saturday, January 31st, this man closed his earthly career in the full assurance of faith He was recognized by the entire community as a godly man who was ready, at all times, to give a reason for the hope that was in him He was, as a matter of course, from what has been already said, an honest man in his business He was a man of far more than ordinary intelligence, and could ex-

press his views with great clearness and calmness, and could support his opinions by reason and logic which were almost irresistible. He never held any half formed opinions on any subject, and in short he was an extraordinary man physically, intellectually and morally, such as few communities can produce. He, at one time in his youth, before the temperance question was agitated or understood, carried on a distillery near Pleasant Unity in this county. But as soon as he begun to examine into and think over the effects of the business upon the community, he abandoned it at once and forever, and for near fifty years he was a most determined foe to the whiskey traffic in all its forms, and an uncompromising and zealous friend of temperance. At the same time, he, for about the same period, was an abolitionist—the given friend of the down trodden and oppressed colored race. He was none of your modern abolitionists, but one of the original brand, who was not afraid to espouse the cause of the oppressed when such espousal was very unpopular. He never was an expediency man, but when satisfied that the thing was *right* he sustained it, and when satisfied it was *wrong* he condemned and opposed it.

He was a firm, zealous and consistent member of the M. E. Church from his youth to the day of his death. Not many weeks since he paid a visit to our town and, as if he had a presentiment that it would be his last visit to Greensburg, although he said nothing about it, he went from house to house and made a personal visit to those with whom he had long been acquainted. He was not afraid to die, but expressed his readiness to depart and be with Christ, which was far better than remaining in this world. He was physically a powerful man, being six feet three or four inches in height, and well proportioned, and remained as erect and straight as a statue. For fifty years or more he was the leading business man in Blairsville. During the time when

the old Pennsylvania Canal was in operation, he was largely engaged in the commission and forwarding business. His death will create a vacuum in the church, in the State and in the community which will not soon be filled by one of like character.

OBITUARY.

LUCY GRAFF, wife of John Graff of Blairsville, Pa., died March 4, 1877, aged 71 years. She was born in Baltimore, Md., October 19, 1805. She was a member of the German Reformed Church for a number of years. She joined the M. E. Church in 1838, of which she continued a consistent member, until death. She died in the triumph of a "living faith," and "her children rise up and call her blessed." She was a woman of decidedly domestic habits, a meek and quiet spirit delighting in the prosperity of her neighbors and annoying none. Herself surrounded by the comforts of a sumptuous home, she labored to make her abundance a blessing to all whose misfortunes brought them under her notice, and many were the blessings invoked upon her by those whose necessity she relieved. Her religion made her life a constant sunshine. She was a model mother, and the "idol" of her children. Never was a family more devoted and assiduous in their attentions than were they, during her illness. Her sufferings were severe and protracted, and yet she never murmured nor complained. She was not only uncomplaining, but even cheerful, during almost her entire sickness. She was greatly interested in the salvation of her children and grandchildren, and it was one of her last acts to impress them with the necessity of preparation for heaven.

No one has passed from this community for years, who was more universally respected than sister Graff. Full of years and good works her life was like a rose, fragrant and beautiful while

here, and now, that she is dead and gone, her acts remain as a testimony in this community to the power of the faith which she professed.

Obituary of James G. Graff

James G., son of John and Lucy Graff, was born January —, 1841, and fell asleep in Jesus on Friday morning the 11th of May, 1860, at half-past seven o'clock.

James was converted at a protracted meeting in Blairsville in the Winter of 1857, but did not hold fast his profession. He remained in a backslidden state until the night of the 23rd of March last, when, becoming greatly concerned about his soul, he called his father to his bedside and requested him to pray. The father, with true parental feeling and solicitude, exhorted the son to unite with him in prayer, which he did in a very earnest and emphatic manner. This exercise was not continued long until he embraced Christ by faith, and was led into the liberty of the Gospel. This happy transition from darkness into the marvelous light of reconciling love was hailed with rejoicing and triumph by himself and parents, whom he tenderly embraced, exclaiming "Now I can die!" From that time until his death he had great peace of mind, and spoke of dying with as much calmness as if he were preparing for only a short journey and temporary absence from home.

A few days before his death, although encouraged by his physician, he began to make distribution of his effects, charging his mother what to do with them. He continued to rise at about five in the morning, and attend to many little things about the house, and to ride out a few miles in the afternoons when the weather was favorable, up to the day next preceding his death, and was only then prevented by the wetness of the day

The evening before he left us, he said he felt that he could not live but a few days, and desired to have the family all together that he might talk to them before his strength should be too much wasted. He expressed a strong desire to see his three brothers converted, and the last efforts of his waning life were put forth for the accomplishment of his laudable wish. As the brothers were kneeling before him, earnestly engaged in prayer, James commanded silence and in a full and animated voice instructed and encouraged them, and spoke of the necessity of the full surrender of their hearts to God. The scene was truly interesting and affecting. There were the assembled family, the kneeling young men overwhelmed with weeping, and the disease-wasted brother, hovering over the border of the spirit world, exhorting them to lay hold by faith, of the atoning sacrifice of Christ. He was soon after consecrated to God by holy baptism, and retired, but rested poorly. At about one in the morning he said to his father: "I think I shall not live more than a few days, but I feel much better; tell mother to take some rest—she is wearing herself out." As he wiped the cold, clammy sweat from his child's brow, the sorrowing father perceived that his end was fast approaching, and told him he could live only a few hours, and asked him how he felt in view of meeting death so soon. An unearthly smile played over his worn countenance, and he said: "I am happy, happy, happy! I feel that I have not served the Lord long enough, but I am happy." As the family approached the bedside, at the sound of every footstep he would turn his head to see who was coming, and pressing their hands and kissing them, he exhorted them all to meet him in heaven, and after receiving their promise, said: "All is well." Observing his mother's grief, he said with tenderness: "Mother, do not mourn for me; I am only going a little before you, and then it will not be long till we shall strike glad hands in heaven."

His vital energies now began rapidly to give way, his vocal powers failed entirely, and it became painfully evident that his hearing was growing dull, but his calm, deep, spiritual eyes slightly elevated and fixed in steady gaze, as if peering through the gathering shades, and resting with delight upon the bright scenes beyond, gave indubitable evidence that consciousness and reason were unimpaired. As the receding billow was slowly bearing him away from the shore of time, the question was propounded, "Do you now feel the presence and sustaining grace of the Saviour?" And though the tongue had lost the power of articulation, the wasted hand was raised, according to request, in token of assent. He gave no signs of suffering, and so gradual and gentle was his departure that the precise moment of the spirit's exit was scarcely discernible.

On Saturday afternoon, notwithstanding the surcharged clouds were pouring the teeming rain upon the earth, a large concourse of people assembled to pay the last tribute of respect to one they loved, and proceeded in solemn procession to the Village Cemetery, whence, after the precious remains had been committed to the grave in sure and certain hope of a part in the first resurrection, forming in procession, they escorted the bereaved relatives back to the family residence.

Thus died one who loved and was kind to every one, and whom everybody loved and respected in return.

"He being dead yet speaketh." J. W. S.

VI.—MARGARET GRAFF.

MARGARET GRAFF, the third daughter of John and Barbara Graff, was born May 3d, 1802, died March 24th, 1885 She was married to John Colleasure, born 1800, died Dec 25th, 1875 They are both buried at Doddsville, Illinois Children

No 1—LUCETTA HAYMAKER, born Oct 10th, 1826, died Aug 22d, 1876 She was married to Irwin Rutledge (who was born Feb 24th, 1826) Oct 23d, 1851 Eight children

(1) LUCY GRAFF, born Nov 10th, 1852, died Sep 30th, 1853
(2) MARGARET JANE, " April 5th, 1854, " Feb 15th, 1855
(3) AUGUSTA EDSON, " Jan 13th, 1856, "
(4) LIZZY ROBERTS, " Apr 23rd, 1858, " Aug 24th, 1874
(5) WILLIAM GRAFF, " Mar 30th, 1860, " " 1st, 1876
(6) FRANK AGNEW, " " 5th, 1862, " 1867
(7) IRWIN, JR, " Dec 9th, 1863
(8) JOHN COLLEASURE, born April 12th, 1865

No 2—ELIZABETH, born June 1828, married Nov 18th, 1852, to Alexander Y Barkley. Ten children

(1) LUCETTA P., born married I C Tomb, June 28th, 1883 Their child Howard was born Sept 26th, 1884

(2) ANNA M, born Jan 1856, married George W Rutlege, Dec 21st, 1882

(3) BABY, born March 1858, died Aug 1858

(4) LIRRIE, " Aug 1860, died 1865

(5) MAGGIE, " "

ouisa C, born July		1862
...ia C,	" "	1864
Wm Frank, "	Aug	1866

No. 3 Margaret Colleasure, Born July 1 1835.

Married Mr. Benj. D. Christy in July 21 1866. died Dec 9, 1885

No. 4 William Colleasure, Born May 21 1840. enlisted in co. C. 119. Ills Aug 9. 1862 dis June 29 1865.

Married Oct 2 in 1877. To L. C Hamilton Dec 31 1876 — 2 children C. W. born Sept [illegible] March [illegible] E Goff b. May 21/83 d.

No. 5 Caroline Colleasure, Born 1842.

Married Mr. Wm Black. Oct 2 1879.

Children. Margaret G. born Nov 8 1860. Wm Plummer born Sept 20 18[illegible]

Three died in Infancy,

Making nine children of

John and Margaret Colleasure.

The above was overlooked.

...n duty He was a young man given to prayer, a regular ...t upon the means of grace, but seldom absent from the ...eeting, always in the Sabbath School, unless providenti...lered, supporting the cause of Christ both by his influence ...ns He engaged in every good word and work, and ...ought to he upon his dying bed, that Saviour whom he ...d religion that he professed did not forsake him

...he had a strong desire to live, as would be very natural ...son of his age, yet as he drew nearer his end, his faith

(6) LOUISA C., born July 1862
(7) ELLA C., " " 1864
(8) WM. FRANK, " Aug. 1866
(9) JENNIE A., " Dec. 1869
(10) EDWARD GRAFF, born Sept. 1872

No. 3.—JAMES, no date of birth given, died Feb. 25th, 1876, aged 28 years 9 months and 17 days.

OBITUARY OF JAMES COLLEASURE.

DIED at his residence near Doddsville, the 25th of February, at 2.40 P. M., of typhoid fever, JAMES COLLEASURE, aged 28 years, 9 months and 17 days.

He was the youngest son of Elder John Colleasure (who was himself suddenly called to his rest on Christmas morning, just two months before), and was a young man of most excellent Christian character. He made a profession of his faith in Christ in the Presbyterian Church of Doddsville, January 26, 1867, under the ministry of Rev. James T. Bliss, and was admitted to membership in that church. His was no empty profession; no sooner was he received into the church than he entered upon active Christian duty. He was a young man given to prayer, a regular attendant upon the means of grace, but seldom absent from the prayer-meeting, always in the Sabbath School, unless providentially hindered, supporting the cause of Christ both by his influence and means. He engaged in every good word and work, and when brought to lie upon his dying bed, that Saviour whom he loved and religion that he professed did not forsake him.

While he had a strong desire to live, as would be very natural for a person of his age, yet as he drew nearer his end, his faith

appeared to grow brighter and stronger When told on the morning before he died, by a member of the church, that he could not live, it produced no excitement He calmly said that he was prepared to go, if it was the Lord's will, and asked that his Sabbath School class might be sent for They came around his bedside at 1 o'clock, at that time he was not able to talk to them, but recognizing them he took them severally by the hand, when Mr Pollock, feeling what their teacher wanted to say to them, told them to be good boys, love their Saviour and prepare to meet their teacher in heaven

While he was at home in all religious services the Sabbath School was his great delight For thirteen months before his death, and how much longer the writer does not know, he was not absent one day from his class And while we sorrow that we shall see him no more on earth, and that he cannot come to us, we rejoice that if we are faithful we shall see him in that better world where sickness and death are not known, and where Jesus walks in the midst of his people

His funeral was the largest ever held in the neighborhood, and had a stranger been present he would have said, from the concourse of people come together, surly a good man has fallen The old church was full to overflowing The funeral discourse was preached by Rev H C Mullen, from 2 Timothy, 1 10, last clause, after which the remains were deposited in the cemetery north of the village, beside his father, there to await the resurrection morning when he shall come forth and be numbered with those of the first resurrection, and so be forever with the Lord

At a congregational meeting the day after he was taken sick, he was elected to take his father's place in the Eldership by an almost unanimous vote, but did not live to be installed

Let his young associates follow him as he followed Christ, so it may be also well with you when you come to die. H B

Obituary of Mr John Colleasure

Died at Doddsville, December 25, 1875, Mr John Colleasure, in the 76th year of his age

Mr Colleasure was born in Kentucky, and at a very early age made his home in Westmoreland County, Pa Here the greater part of his life was spent. In 1824 he was married to Miss Margaret Graff, and together they traveled the journey of life down to the time of his death He united with the Presbyterian Church at Mt Pleasant in 1829, then under the pastoral care of Rev Patterson He was elected to the office of ruling elder in 1838 in which he has served the church ever since He moved to Illinois in 1857, where he immediately found work to do for the Master in the churches of New Providence and Doddsville, where his efficiency as an elder and his piety as a Christian will not soon be forgotten Elder Colleasure, as a Christian, was a living epistle, read and known of all men, and his humble, meek and blameless life was mighty in building up the cause of religion, for the world saw in him a living testimony for Jesus Therefore the church and community feel that in his removal they have sustained a great loss Elder Colleasure loved the Sabbath School, and it was his heart's delight to labor in it He was a most faithful teacher of a Bible class, for many years, till a few months before his death, when, on account of his failing strength, he gave it into other hands, yet he seldom failed to meet with them The last year of his life he was absent but *one* Sabbath

The end of his earthly life was evidently that of one who felt that he was nearing home He spent much of his time in memorizing the Scriptures and the singing of favorite hymns, such as, "On Jordan's stormy banks I stand," and "Come, we that love the Lord" He loved the Lord, and the Lord showed His love to him by taking him to Himself without lingering pain

and suffering One of the most prominent traits in his Christian character was his unshaken confidence in God He never gave way to gloom or despondency When adversity came he never seemed to be cast down or troubled, but confidently trusted that the Lord would do all things well, and with child-like faith he clung closer to God Like Moses he finished his work faithfully, and the Lord took him gently to Himself

On Christmas eve he attended an entertainment in the church for the benefit of the Sabbath School, made an earnest and solemn prayer at its opening, and took a lively interest in the proceedings of the evening Alas! how little we thought that it would be his last prayer

He went home, and after a secret prayer, at his bedside, of more than ordinary length, he retired in his usual health

He slept soundly till five o'clock in the morning, when the Master called He rose up in the bed, spoke of a strange feeling in his breast, but immediately lay down, and before the members of his family could be summoned to his bedside, his spirit had gone from its house of clay to be forever with the Lord, whom so ardently he had loved and so faithfully had followed

He was the father of nine children, three died in infancy The remainning six he lived to see members of the Presbyterian Church, who, with his aged companion, still live to mourn the loss of a kind husband and an affectionate father, whose godly example they will ever remember till they shall meet him, with songs of joy, in the Father's house above, and the church at Doddsville will long remember him as a faithful and earnest leader, whose Christian life is worthy of imitation H C MULLAN

OBITUARY OF MRS JOHN COLLTASURE

MRS MARGARET COLLTASURE was born May 6, 1802, and died at the home of her daughter near Doddsville, Illinois, March 24

1885 She was the sister of Jacob Graff and Mrs Elizabeth Armstrong, who are generally known In 1824 she was married to John Colleasure in Pennsylvania, and in 1857 they removed to Illinois and settled in Schuyler county Theirs was a happy life Nine children were born to them of whom some are yet living On Christmas morn, 1875, the husband and father passed to his reward Early in life her mind was turned to sacred things by a prayer-book presented to her by a minister of the Gospel She united with the Presbyterian Church of Pleasant Unity in 1829 Though several years elapsed between the time of her conversion and her union with the church, yet they were not misspent Unassuming, almost to a fault she manifested in her daily life the religion she professed She lived not for herself but for her friends and family For several years she had been a sufferer from asthma This seemed to have developed into congestion of the lungs a few weeks preceding her death Her nights were spent in intense suffering, but with coming of day, her suffering would diminish She seemed to feel that her end was near Her faith would reach up beyond things earthly and give her glimpses of the celestial city Her death was peaceful and painless "See! see!" she whispered to her children and friends as they gathered around her bedside They were angels who had come to carry her home She gently closed her eyes and fell asleep in Jesus

The funeral services were held in the Presbyterian Church at Doddsville A large number of friends and neighbors assembled to pay their last tribute of love and esteem After a very appropriate sermon her remains were laid to rest by the side of those of her husband in the Doddsville Cemetery Well can we say, "O death, where is thy sting, O grave, where is thy victory?"

VII.—JOSEPH GRAFF

JOSEPH GRAFF, the fifth son of John and Barbara Graff, was born Oct 13, 1804, and died in 1806 He was buried on the Bash farm, near Pleasant Unity, where his father and mother were afterwards buried

---

VIII.—ELIZABETH GRAFF

ELIZABETH, the fourth daughter of John and Barbara Graff, was born Jan 7, 1806, died May 19, 1888, in Doddsville, Ill, and was buried at Rushville On Feb 10, 1831, she was married to John Armstrong, who was born Jan 4 1808, and died Dec 29, 1882 He also was buried at Rushville Mrs Armstrong was a member of the M E Church for 46 years. She was a devoted Christian and much given to prayer On her deathbed she prayed for her departure that she might be with Christ and also for the dear ones left behind Her husband, John Armstrong, was a very industrious man He had no educational advantages in early life He was a strong advocate of temperance and was one of the first men in Westmoreland County to join the temperance society This was in 1829 He was also very benevolent and never turned the needy away

Children and Grandchildren

No 1—Caroline, born Sept 10, 1832, married to Edgar A Burnham, May 4, 1858 Children

(1)	John A.,	born Feb 4 1859
(2)	Frank P	" April 17, 1860
(3)	Elizabeth	" March 17, 1863, married Wm [R Clugston, Feb 13, 1889
(4)	Edgar,	" Oct 3, 1864
(5)	A L.,	" Jan 12, 1866 died Sep. 5, 1867
(6)	Minnie,	" Jan 16, 1868
(7)	Paul Graff,	" Jan 18, 1869
(8)	Hannah,	" April 10, 1870
(9)	Kate,	" Nov 19, 1871
(10)	Annie,	" March 23, 1873
(11)	Albert Carpenter,	" April 3, 1874
(12)	Fred William,	" Oct 8, 1875

No 2—Priscilla, the second daughter of John and Elizabeth Armstrong was born Oct 14, 1838, is unmarried and living at Doddsville, Illinois

IX.—PETER GRAFF.

PETER GRAFF, the fifth son of John and Barbara Graff, was born on the farm in Westmoreland county, Pa., May 27, 1808, and died, April 9, 1890.

His early childhood was spent amid the stirring scenes of the War of 1812. He distinctly remembered the gathering of the soldiers in his neighborhood, as they were starting for the scene of war. He was too young at the time to fully realize what it meant, and when he saw the weeping and lamentation at the parting of those brave men from their friends, he could not understand it. As the war progressed, its horrors made a lasting impression on his memory.

His early education was limited, as country schools, in those days, were few and only opened in the winter months while pupils had often long distances to go. He mentions one of his teachers as being the father of Gov. Geary. He was full of energy, and this showed itself early in life. At about sixteen years of age, his brother, Henry, gave him a situation in his store at Pleasant Unity, Westmoreland County, Pa., where he remained about two years. Then his brother gave him for several years charge of a branch store in New Derry. This was afterwards sold. He was married to Susanna Lobengier, in Westmoreland County, January 25, 1830. His business qualifications developed so strongly, that he

and his brother Henry commenced business in Blairsville, for the sale of general merchandise The style of the firm was H and P Graff

During the five or six years that he remained in Blairsville, Indiana County, Pa, he became a very popular merchant His business increased so rapidly that he was compelled to employ five or six clerks to do it Many customers bringing produce over thirty miles to exchange for merchandise He was a thoughtful and clear-headed young man, being only about twenty five or six years old at this time They formed a partnership with Messrs E G Dutilh & Co, commission merchants of Philadelphia, to transport merchandise from Philadelphia and Baltimore to Pittsburgh and further West The name of the Company was called the Union Transportation Line Before his departure, in 1836, to Pittsburgh, many friends gathered around him to say good by and also to congratulate him on the successful and responsible position he was about to take charge of, the agent for the Union Transportation Line, of which he was a large shareholder, to receive and forward merchandise and produce east and west

During his residence in Pittsburgh, he became a partner in the firm of J Painter & Co, wholesale grocers His business interests so increased in the manufacturing of iron, in Armstrong, Venango and Clarion Counties, that he was obliged, in 1844, to move his residence to Buffalo Mills, Armstrong County, Pa, where he resided until his death

In 1840, he became a Christian, and connected himself with the Lutheran Church. This was a joyful event to his dear old mother, who had prayed so many years for his conversion, and she wrote him a very beautiful letter, which is copied in the short history of her life. With his profession of Christianity, a new life sprang up, new aims grew and developed for Christ! As in business, he was infused with the same spirit of energy in his Christian life. *Fifty years* he was Superintendant of the Sabbath School, fifty years one of the principal men of the church, fifty years working, instructing, giving, and walking with God, until his death! What an epitaph to leave for his children and his friends! And in memory of this noble life—now in God's hands—my prayer is, that it may be the means of leading many souls to seek an interest in Christ, and to follow in the footsteps of this faithful servant of the Lord!

THE CHILDREN OF PETER AND SUSANNA GRAFF

No. 1—JOSEPH, born July 17th, 1831. He married Miss Jane Reynolds in Kittanning, Pa. They had five children, Alexander, Ross Reynolds, Edmund, Susie Lobrigier, and Jane Reynolds.

(1) ALEXANDER married Mary L. Truby, June 5, 1884. Children:

ANDREW DUFF, born April 23rd, 1885.
ANNA MUSGRAVE, " Dec. 24th, 1886.
CHARLES HENRY, " Jan. 23rd, 1890.

(2) SUSAN L., married Andrew C. Bailey, March 18th, 1886. Children:

ROSS REYNOLDS, born Mar. 4th, 1887.
JEAN MOSS ROSS, " June 4th, 1888.

Cyrus [illegible]. Linton, who married Sara Jane,

Died April 21st., 1891.

No 2—MARY LOBINGIER, born, Feb 17th, 1834, died Mar, 4th, 1842, aged 8 years

No 3—ANNA BARBARA, born Aug 31st, 1836 Died April 21 1891

She was married to Wm H Kirkpatrick Nov 25th, 1859, at Buffalo Mills, Armstrong Co, Pa No children Now living in Allegheny City, Pa

No 4—ELIZABETH, born Jan 25th, 1840, died Mar 24th, 1842

No 5—CHAS HUMPHRIES, born May 4, 1842 died Sep 2, 1842

No 6—SARAH JANE, born Aug 3d, 1843

Married to Cyrus B Linton, Buffalo Mills, Pa, Oct 31st, 1878 They have one child, Edmund Graff, born Sept 2nd, 1879 The family live at Clifton Springs, N Y, where Mr Linton is business manager of the Sanatarium

No 7—EDMUND DUFILH, born Aug 14th, 1846

Unmarried, makes his home with his parents at Buffalo Mills, Pa.

No 8—PHILIP MELANCHTHON, born Aug 15th, 1848

Married Sarah Agnes Earhart Oct 15th, 1872, at Worthington, Armstrong Co, Pa They have five children Anna Barbara, Margaret Gertrude, Carroll Friedt, Agnes Virginia and Herbert Hovey, and now reside in Duluth, Minn

No 9—PETER, born June 24th, 1851

Married Hattie O'Brien Oct 12th, 1880, in Brooklyn, N Y No children Reside at Utica, New York

No 10—CHARLES HENRY, born Nov 10, 1854, died Sep 29, 1889

Unmarried and practiced medicine in Duluth, Minn He was thoroughly educated, and took a high rank in his profession, also was highly esteemed, as the following tributes show

Gone to His Rest

Chas H Graff was born and brought up at Kitanning, Pa, and would have been 35 years old had he lived until November He graduated from Gettysburg college in 1876, and from the medical department of the University of Pennsylvania in 1879 The following two years he spent in the hospitals of Vienna and the University of Gottingen, coming to Duluth in 1881 Some time afterward he went to Sweden and studied the Swedish language and attended lectures in the city of Stockholm In 1887-8 he spent a year in foreign travel, passing the winter in Egypt and the Holy Land If one word had to be chosen to characterize Dr Graff, that word would be "student" He was an omnivorous reader, and his studies were by no means confined to subjects related to his profession, but ran out along many lines of science, literature and art It might almost be said that he sacrificed his life to his insatiable thirst for knowledge, for many a time after a day spent in the arduous duties of his profession, he has spent the entire night in reading and study, depriving himself of needed rest and using up the strength which might have brought him out a conqueror in the struggle with disease

His father and mother are still living at Kitanning, but unable by reason of their more than 80 years to come and follow their son to the grave. Two brothers, Peter, of Utica, N Y, and Edmund D, of Kitanning are now here, besides Phillip Melanchthon, who resides in Duluth, a younger brother, Frank, from Kitanning, and his sister, Mrs Wm Kirkpatrick, of Pittsburg, are now on the way and expected on Tuesday It has been decided that the burial will be in Duluth, but the time of the funeral will be announced hereafter

He occupied a place in the front ranks of his profession, his great skill, both as a physician and surgeon, made his services

in constant demand The income from his practice, supplemented by wise investments, had gained for him a competence Learned in his profession, cultured in mind, genial in nature, and generous in heart, Dr Graff will be sadly missed and deeply mourned not only by those who are connected with him by ties of blood, but by friends, many and warm Eulogies will be spoken, and a monument reared over his last resting-place, but the truest, grandest tribute which will be paid to the worth of Dr. Graff, will be the tears and blessings of the hundreds of poor, to whom, in sickness or accident, he not only gave freely of his time and skill, but of his means as well, providing for those who were unable to procure them for themselves, the medicines and dainty food that brought them back to health

OBITUARY

Dr C H Graff, a Pennsylvanian, Who Won Distinction and Wealth in Duluth

St Paul, Minn, Sept 29, [Special]—Dr C H Graff, one of the many Pennsylvanians for whose adoption of Minnesota as their home this State has reason to be gratified, died at Duluth this morning at the age of 34 years. He was taken sick a month ago with typhoid fever

Dr Graff had been a resident of Duluth for about nine years, and stood at the very head of the medical fraternity, having a very large practice He graduated in the medical department of the University of Pennsylvania in 1879, and afterwards went to Heidelberg, where he also graduated Twice since he located in Duluth he has been in Europe, studying at both Vienna and Stockholm On one of these visits he made a trip through Italy, Turkey, Egypt and Asia Minor

He was elected coroner of St Louis County, in which Duluth is located, in 1884, by nearly 2,000 majority, running on the Democratic ticket He was always a hard student, reading until 2 or 3 o'clock in the morning after a hard day's work This overwork caused such a weakening of his vital forces that he could not resist the attack of the disease His brother, Phillip Melanchthon Graff, is a resident of Duluth, and his brothers, Ed D Graff, of Pennsylvania, and Peter Graff, of Utica, N Y, are now in Duluth, while another brother and a sister are on the way Dr Graff was never married He leaves a large amount of property, mostly in real estate and other investments, in Duluth and the vicinity

A Professorship Endowed

Special Telegram to the *Times*

Gettysburg, Oct 31 —Peter Graff, of Worthington, has announced the gift of $25,000 out of the estate of his son, Charles H Graff, M D, who died recently in Duluth, Minn, to endow a professorship in Pennsylvania College at Gettysburg, to be known as "The Dr Charles H Graff Professorship of Hygiene and Physical Culture" Dr George D Staley, of Lebanon, formerly of Harrisburg, has been chosen to fill the chair

No 11 —John Francis, born Aug 12th, 1857

Married Carrie Louise Brown, Dec 27th, 1881, in Lancaster, Pa They live at Buffalo Mills, Pa Children

(1) James Brown, born Dec 21st, 1882
(2) Peter, " Sept 15th, 1886
(3) John Francis, " Dec 28th, 1888
(4) Mary Hay Graff, born Sept 25th, 1890

A Brief Sketch of the Life and Work of Peter Graff

From the Kittanning *Globe*

The news of the death of the venerable citizen whose name precedes this mention is already probably well known throughout the country. He was a conspicuous figure among the generation of men now rapidly passing away, and in the course of more than half a century of active business life was so largely identified with the history of the business prosperity of the region in which he lived that his death will be the subject of deep and sincere regret among every class of men that the personality of his large-hearted and generous nature touched.

He was a pioneer among the material beginnings of our prosperity, and while he so largely helped in building the foundations of the industrial enterprises, with which his foresight and business skill were identified, he has built as well a record of an upright, generous and consistent Christian life, that will ever stand as the most enduring monument to his memory.

Mr. Graff commenced his business career in this country sometime in 1844, when with the late Jacob Painter, of Pittsburg, he became the joint owner of the then valuable property known as the Buffalo Furnace, and in the successful management of its affairs up to 1864, he amassed large means.

He was afterward concerned in the establishment and management of the Buffalo woolen mills, one of the most

prominent and successful business concerns in the country, and upon the discovery of oil in the upper country, through fortunate investments, he became the possessor of large tracts of land that returned immense income. Through all these different channels into which his sagacious foresight and business ability were cast, he accumulated large means that placed him in the rank of the very wealthy men of the country.

In the abounding generosity of his nature his wealth has been made the source of much good and benefaction. Devoutly attached to the tenets of the Lutheran faith he was an active and consistent member of the congregation of that denomination in Worthington near where he lived, and gave very largely of his means toward its support. At the erection of the new and beautiful edifice of worship, of that body, he contributed by far the greater amount of the fund necessary to its erection, and it was not only in his giving that his influence was felt, but more in the active, earnest and devoted Christian life that he led, as an exemplar of the noblest characteristics of a Christian manhood.

For more than forty years he was the Superintendent of the Sabbath School of that thriving congregation, instilling into the growing minds the precepts of religious truth and giving bent and direction to the moral growth of the entire community.

He lived not only within, but somewhat beyond the confines of his dogmatic faith in the religion of good deeds, of character, of sincerity, in honest endeavor, of

cheerful hope, and above all in a religion for every day in the giving of food and raiment to the deserving objects of help. The religion of health and happiness, freedom and content. In the religion of work, and in the ceremonies of honest labor. Such a life was a potent factor for good in its own showing, and leaves behind it an impulse toward moral achievement, a halo of departing light that shall long give direction to those that strive.

He was the sympathizing friend to the whole community who trusted to his larger experience, counsel and help, in moments of doubt, distress or darkened light, and as was eloquently said by the servant man of God who pronounced the last tribute of regard before the temple of his great heart was lowered to the grave, "if all whom his helping hand assisted could have been present at his funeral, it would have been the largest ever seen in the country."

His munificent donation to the Lutheran College at Gettysburg, recently bestowed, and the ample charities that in every direction have flowed from his hands during his life time, and that will probably be remembered in the disposition of his large estate, make his death one of the most significant, in its relations not only to the present but to the future, that have taken place in the county.

Above his silent clay, as it was consigned to earth last Friday afternoon, many sorrowing tears were shed by old and young, rich and poor, kinsman and neighbor, for whom the loving heart had forever ceased to beat, whose busy brain was still, and from whose hand had dropped the sacred torch.

THE following funeral sermon was preached by the Rev J W Schwartz, for many years Mr Graff's pastor:

TEXT.—2 Samuel 3 38—"*Know ye not that there is a prince and a great man fallen this day in Israel?*"

A brief glance at the history of the event referred to here will help us to understand the text more clearly

After the death of Saul, the first king of Israel, when David undertook to set up his throne as king—Abner, Captain of Saul's host, resisted his authority, and set up Ish-bosheth, Saul's son, to reign in Saul's stead The result of this rivalry was a battle between David's subjects, led by Joab, and Ish-bosheth's, under command of Abner This battle ended disastrously to Abner's forces, for many were slain and the rest fled Asahel, one of Joab's brothers, pursued Abner to kill him, and he (Abner), in self-defence, slew his pursuer. Not long after this, Abner withdrew his allegience from Ish-bosheth and made a treaty of peace with David, and, in an interview with him, made a covenant to be his subject thenceforth forever When he left David's presence, Joab—no doubt through revenge for Asahel's death—treacherously slew him David, when he heard this, mourned bitterly for Abner, and called on his people to mourn with him, and the words of our text are a part of the lamentation he uttered In these words he meant to say that Abner's death—not merely because of the way in which it had been accomplished, but because of his qualities as a leader—was a cause of mourning to all the people

The theme this subject suggests for our study to-day is, THE DEATH OF PROMINENT MEN A SORE BEREAVEMENT TO THE COMMUNITY IN WHICH THEY LIVED

As a rule, when any one dies, that death brings sorrow to *some* hearts, however few. Now and then, there are those who leave the world "unwept, unhonored and unsung," but they are comparatively few. Many, when they die, leave behind a large circle of loving hearts, bound to them by tender ties of kinship, that are sorely stricken when these ties are broken But, now and then, one dies, whose relations to the whole neighborhood around him have been such that all mourn his loss. This last class is the one we are considering to-day In our discussion of this subject, let us consider what are the qualities that are necessary to entitle one to the name, "a great man," "a prince "

In general, it may be said, *they are those that make a man worthy of the esteem of his fellow-men*—qualities that *eminently fit* him to be a leader among men A man is not great merely because he happens to occupy a place of honor, or wealth If he is great, it is because he deserves these distinctions

These qualities are, a strict moral integrity, sound worldly wisdom, diligence in one's vocation, a heart full of sympathy for others and a true Christian character.

Let us dwell on these qualities a little while, that we may see what meaning they have

(*a*) *Strict moral integrity* By this is meant a sincere love for what is right, *because it is right*, and not merely

for the sake of the worldly gain it will bring It includes a character free from vicious habits, honesty in our dealings with our fellow-men and being what we seem to others to be, as we mingle with them

(*b*) *Sound worldly wisdom* By this is meant not necessarily a large amount of worldly learning, but the ability to make the best use of whatever knowledge one possesses, be it much or little It includes an accurate judgment—the power to see clearly what objects are worth striving for, and what right means are best fitted to secure those objects.

(*c*) *Diligence in one's vocation.* This means that attention that brings him success in it It means a patient perseverance in it, even though amid many discouragements.

(*d*) *A heart full of sympathy for others.* This means a readiness to share in the joys and sorrows of others, and especially in their sorrows, and to be ready to relieve the distress of others, even though it cost great self-denial

(*e*) *A true Christian character.* Do you need to be told what is meant by this? What else *can* it mean but a sincere love for God and earnest desire to serve him, a humble, hearty confession of one's sinfulness, and a firm faith in Jesus Christ as his only Saviour from sin and its consequences

Now, he who possesses these qualities is truly great, no matter what his station in life is, and the more they abound in him, the more Prince-like is his character.

Now, the death of such men is sore bereavement to the community in which they lived For,

1st Each person in the community feels such a death to be a personal loss No one can long live a life like this without finding abundant opportunity to help others prosper, and in countless ways he will confer benefits on others that will fill them with sincere gratitude to him. Beside this, many who are not under obligations to him for favors received, will be filled with the kindest regard for the noble qualities they see in him, and so are led to cherish warm personal friendship for him He will seem dear to them, almost, as one of their own kin, and so his death will seem a personal loss

2nd. When such men die, it is not very easy to fill their place

3rd The world has none too many men of this kind, at the most, and instead of the number decreasing, it should be increased

There can be no question that, with each succeeding generation the wants of the human race are rapidly increasing in every direction ; and each successive age calls more and more loudly for men of large heart, and brain, and energy, and influence, and means, to study these wants and devise the best means to meet them And when men of this kind are found, how the world clings to them! and when they die, what a vacant place they leave! And, now, is this a suitable occasion for the utterance of such sentiments? There is no question that it is When *any* event of more than ordinary import-

ance occurs, it is the part of wisdom to seek to learn some profitable lesson from it, and when one who has occupied an eminent place in the community dies, it is very profitable to study his life and see what of good that study will bring.

It is not with any desire to flatter that I point to the career of Brother Graff, and ask, What has made his life the success it has been? What is it that has given him the financial standing, the social influence, the religious reputation he has had these many years? He did not begin life with these advantages. Many a time he has said to me that he began life with comparatively nothing How then, does it come that his name has been so prominent for so long a time?

For well nigh fifty years I myself have known him to be intimately connected with important business interests in one place or another. For nearly thirty years I have known much of his reputation as a Christian worker, and for more than twenty years, I have seen how intimately he was associated with nearly all the interests of our community What is the secret of all this? I believe it is to be found in this that he possessed in large measure the qualities already suggested as essential to success in life

His moral character has always been above reproach In his dealings with men, he was at all times reliable In financial affairs, there never was the time when his word was not as good as his bond

His judgment was eminently sound and clear. Many

men sought his counsel in their difficulties, and almost always, when they followed his advice they found the way out of their trouble.

His diligence in business was unsurpassed, and his application, energy and providence went very far to give him the reputation he had to the very end of his life in all business affairs.

But it is of the finer qualities of his nature I delight to speak. What a tender heart he had! How ready he was at all times to minister to those in distress! I have often said that when Brother Graff should die if those, and those only, whom he aided in substantial ways, should all attend his funeral, it would be the largest ever witnessed in our community. His heart always beat in pity for those in trouble, and his hand was ever open to relieve their wants. More than once he has done this at great self-denial—*as I well know.*

And then, as regards his Christian character. Day by day, he realized and confessed himself a poor sinner, deserving nothing good from God but yet trusting with unshaken faith in the atoning work of our Lord for salvation. All here know how repeatedly and earnestly he sought to persuade men to forsake their sinful lives and consecrate themselves to God's service. How it grieved his heart when he saw any spending their time and wasting their strength in sinful pleasure. He delighted in the prosperity of the Church and Sabbath School, and was always ready to give freely in money and work for their success. For over fifty years he has been actively

engaged in Christian work Ever since I have known him, he has been one of the elders in our church here, and nearly all of this time he has been Superintendent of our Sabbath School

And now, does not God design to teach us all a very important lesson in taking him from our midst? Surely He is seeking to bring the church to look out among its membership some one to take his place Is there not some undeveloped talent that may be found and brought into use? It is good for a church, often, to have its earthly props removed, that it may be led to trust in God earnestly, and bring into active use its latent powers. As a community, we can learn *this* lesson .—that, after all, there is nothing that brings richer reward than a life devoted to the service of God and brightest interests of our fellow-men

To his family, God comes in this bereavement with a lesson full of comfort and instruction

You have much to *comfort* you in his life and in his death He died "like one who wraps the drapery of his couch about him, and lies down to pleasant dreams," and he so died, because he lived in unskaken faith in Jesus.

There is much in his life that is worthy of emulation by his children Are there any of you who will take his place in the church? He began to serve the Lord when he was younger than some of you; and see what a record he has left! Why may not you follow him, as he followed Christ, and so help to enlarge his sphere of usefulness, by having him live in your lives?

I assure you of the hearty sympathy of all this vast congregation, and of many who are not here to-day God has sorely bereaved you in this providence. From the wife, in her declining years, He has taken the strong arm on which for three-score years she has so trustingly leaned, from the children he has taken a father whose counsel seemed so helpful He has seen it good to afflict you all so sorely of late But it is all right and after while you will know why He deals with you as He does With all my heart I commend you to His tender care, assuring you with perfect confidence that He has given His angels charge over you, to keep you in all your ways, if you only trust Him

"The Lord bless you and keep you

"The Lord make His face shine upon you, and be gracious unto you

"The Lord lift up His Countenance upon you and give you peace." Amen!

X.—JACOB GRAFF.

JACOB GRAFF, the sixth son of John and Barbara Graff, was born September 5th, 1810, and died, December 9th, 1886. He was married, June 9th, 1836, to Sarah A Pershing who was born June 22d, 1818. He lived with his mother on the farm where he was born until the age of seventeen At this age he learned the trade of making hats—silk, wool, and the finest beaver, with his brother-in-law, John Colleasure, in the village of Pleasant Unity He was very industrious and a good workman, doing business for himself for several years He then moved to New Derry, Westmoreland County, Pa, about ten miles from the County seat, Greensburg, where he was married, and where he engaged in the milling business with Mr Armstrong, his brother-in-law, until he moved to Rushville, Illinois There he purchased a farm and also built a steam flouring mill He continued in that business until a short time before his death

At the age of 22, he became a Christian and united with the Methodist E. Church in Pleasant Unity He was an earnest and faithful follower of Christ. He soon became a class leader in the church and engaged in all Christian work until his death He was one of the four elder sons who were faithful servants of Christ for over fifty years!

The Children of Jacob Graff Wert

No 1—Cyrus, born Oct 27th, 1837

On Feb 18th, 1868, he married Mary C Potts, who was born Oct 15th, 1840 Their children are

(1) Charles W, born Dec 15th, 1868
(2) John P, " May 22d, 1871
(3) Mary M, " June 16th, 1876

No 2—Wilbur F, born Mar 12th, 1840, died Oct 22d, 1862

No 3—John, born Sept 2d, 1842

On March 15th, 1866, he married Hettie Ramsey who was born August 10th, 1840 Their children are

(1) Paul D, born Dec 26th, 1866
(2) Anna M, " Jan or June 6th, 1871
(3) Effie J, " Aug 3rd, 1873
(4) Sarah P, " April 10th 1876
(5) William R, " Oct 26th, 1877
(6) Rhoda, " Sept 16th, 1879

John is now living in Tecumseh, Neb, engaged in dry goods business

No 4—Hiram, born Oct 22d, 1844

On Dec 27th, 1872, he married Sarah E Wilson, who was born Apr 4th, 1847, and died Feb 21st, 1883 Their children are

(1) Herbert W born May 24th, 1874, died Mar 30th, 1878
(2) Wilbur, " July 20th, 1877.
(3) Clarke, " April 20th, 1879
(4) Harold, " June 15th 1881

No 5—Joseph, born Feb 18th, 1848 died Oct 13th 1851

No 6—Edward, born Feb 19th, 1857

THE FOLLOWING OBITUARY NOTICE OF JACOB GRAFF WAS PUBLISHED

On last Thursday morning the people of our city were astonished by the announcement that "Father Graff" was dead And yet every one said the peaceful and quiet way in which he passed away was fitting the life he had lived

Jacob Graff was born in Westmoreland County, Pa., September 5th, 1810, making him 76 years, 3 months, and 4 days old He was converted and joined the Methodist Episcopal Church in his 22d year, and has lived an honored and consistent Christian life from the time of his profession During most of the time he was a class-leader, and has always lived up to the discipline idea of a sub-pastor. He was married to Miss Sarah Pershing, June 9th, 1836, and for fifty years and six months they have walked happily together, and in the nature of the case, it cannot be long until they will be re united where death never comes

Brother Graff came to Rushville in 1853, and lived here as one of our citizens until his death, thus for 33 years he has gone in and out among this people, and many there are who rise up and call him blessed He was not demonstrative or boastful but calm and reserved yet ever anxious and solicitous about the erring or needy, and in his timid, gentle and kind way, went about to do them good His life was akin to the greatest forces of God—the silent ones! Talents may break forth like a

blazing comet and attract attention for a while, wealth may command obeisance and wield a sceptre of power for a season, but after all there is no life that compares with that one which is "hid with Christ in God." The last public service that Father Graff attended was that of a Love Feast followed with the Sacrament of the Lord's Supper. On Thursday morning, December 9th, 1886, he awakened about half past five o'clock, and remarked to his wife that he would arise to begin the duties of another day, but it was only the Spirit that arose, for while speaking he bowed his head and fell back asleep in Jesus. "He was not, for God took him." F. M. Sisson.

The funeral services were conducted at the M. E. Church, by the Pastor, assisted by the Revs. John Clarke and John Knowly. There was a large congregation assembled to pay their last respects to their esteemed fellow citizen. The remains were laid to rest in the Rushville Cemetery, about 4 o'clock, p. m. His sons, Messrs. John Graff, of Tecumseh, Nebraska, and Edward Graff, who is a student at the Wesleyan University, at Bloomington, arrived here in time to attend the obsequies.

XI.—MATTHEW GRAFF

MATTHEW GRAFF, the seventh son of John and Barbara Graff, who was born August 12th, 1812, is still living and now resides near Kensington, Ohio After leaving his mother's home, he clerked for his brother Henry in Pleasant Unity, and learned the business of a country merchant At the age of twenty he went to Blairsville, Indiana County, Pa doing business for his brothers Henry and Peter. In 1836 he was married, having at that time an interest in the business, remaining in the firm until 1852, when he removed to Pittsburgh, and at once engaged in the manufacturing of stoves, castings, etc In 1858 his health failed, and he was obliged to dispose of his business interests in the city He then purchased a farm in Ohio near Kensington, where he now resides

In the year 1838, he became a Christian, and then began the development of this new life in the work of Christ He soon became a leading member of the Lutheran Church He was elected deacon, then elder, he became a teacher in the Sabbath School and engaged in other Christian work After his removal to Pittsburg, he soon became a leading man in the church there—was elected elder, and engaged prominently in all Christian work.

After removing to Ohio—there being no Lutheran

Church in the neighborhood—he at once connected himself with the Presbyterian Church, and so continued his Christian work. He was soon elected a ruling elder, and is still an active worker for Christ, having thus far, walked with God for over fifty years!

In a letter he says, "I well remember the trip we made in bringing our grandparents in the cold winter month to our home near Pleasant Unity, in a two horse wagon over rough, bad roads A terrible journey for such old people"

On January 18th, 1836, he was married to Barbara Lobengier, who was born January 10th, 1814.

CHILDREN AS FOLLOWS

No 1—HENRY C., born April 29th, 1838

No 2—AUG. B., " Dec. 5th, 1840, has two children living

No 3—FRANK M., " Aug 29th, 1842, one child

No 4—SEBASTIAN C., " Jan 10th, 1844, six children

No 5—ELIZABETH, " Mar 14th, 1846; died Mar 17th, 1846

No 6—EDWARD E., " Feb 1st, 1850

No 7—RICHARD K., " Oct 14th, 1853, died Sept 9th, 1856.

No 8.—MARY E., " June 7th, 1857

She married Geo R Thompson, have one child

No 9—LIDA B., born Jan 1st, 1860 She married

XII.—PAUL GRAFF.

PAUL GRAFF, the eighth son of John and Barbara Graff, was born May 31st, 1815

On January 21st, 1841, he was married to Rebecca Trimble, who was born Oct. 9th, 1822 Children as follows:

No 1—ALBERT, born Oct 21st, 1841

On Nov 19th, 1868, he was married to Jennie M Audenried, who was born Dec 31st, 1843 Three children

(1) ISABELLA A., born May 6th, 1870
(2) REBECCA TRIMBLE, " Nov 5th, 1872
(3) ANNA AUDENRIED, " July 27th, 1879

No 2—JAMES T, born May 22d, 1843

On April 27th, 1871, he was married to Susie E Aumont, who was born Sept 10th, 1847, died Sept 28th, 1877 Two children

(1) JAMES AUMONT, born Aug 10th, 1872, died,
(2) EDGAR PAUL, " Oct 30th, 1876

No 3—CUYLER, born Nov 11th, 1844, died Dec 7th, 1846

No 4—CLARA E, " Sept 16th, 1852

No 5—PAUL FRANCIS," March 1st, 1857, died Oct 31st, 1859

After collecting and recording the facts relating to the Graff Family, I think it but right that I should give a short sketch of my own life, from boyhood to the present date, 1890, so far as I can recollect

After my father's death, which occurred December, 1818, when I was not quite 4 years old, my home was with my mother brothers and sisters on the farm in Westmoreland County, Pa I went to school but little, and then only in the winter months, until the age of 12 years. Of course, my education was limited, having to do my share of work—or what I was able, on the farm, such as feeding the stock, carrying water to the reapers and mowers, also raking and making hay, etc At the age of 14, my brother John purchased the store of my brother Henry, located in Pleasant Unity, and he gave me a situation therein I was to sell goods, sweep and keep the store in order, and make myself generally useful. For all this, I was to receive sixty dollars and board per year—furnishing my own clothes

I remained in this small village for several years, then I went to Blairsville, Indiana County, to be with my brothers, Henry and Peter I was employed first in their store, and then in the warehouse, altogether about eight years. In 1840 I accepted a clerkship in Hollidaysburgh, Blair County, in the Union Transportation Line It was at this time that I was engaged to be married, and in January 21st, 1841, I was married to Miss Rebecca Trimble, of Blairsville. After this important event in my life, I commenced business for myself, at Hollidaysburgh, in partnership with Mr William M. Lloyd, in a store of general merchandise, Mr Lloyd at that time being agent for the Union Transportation Line. I continued in business with Mr Lloyd until 1853—twelve years

I then went to Philadelphia in the autumn of 1853, and in the spring of 1854, I commenced in Philadelphia the wholesale boot and shoe business, in partnership with Messrs Darling & Elliott, on Third street above Arch After changing the firm two or three times, we moved to 512 Market street, in 1873, the style of the firm being Graff, Son & Co The firm still remains the same, with no change of partners I have built a new store on the old premises, which was occupied August, 1890

It was during my residence in Hollidaysburgh, in the year 1843, that I united with the Presbyterian Church, Rev. Dr David McKinney Pastor

I consider this to be one of the most important steps in my life, and I trust I became a true child of God What a happy change to take up the Cross and follow the Lamb of God! I was the youngest son of an aged Christian mother, who had spent many hours in prayer by day and by night, for the conversion of her son It has been a great regret to me that my dear mother died two years previous to my conversion What would have been her joy, had she been living, to have seen the result of her faithfulness, and God's answer to prayer! What must have been her rejoicing with the angels in Heaven over her son's repentance, as we are assured in Holy Scripture that even the Angels rejoice over every soul returning to God!

In the course of the year, after my uniting with the Church, I engaged in Christian work as a Sabbath School teacher and was soon after elected a deacon I remained

a member of the Presbyterian church in Hollidaysburg, Pa., until the year 1853 We then removed to Philadelphia, when my wife, who was also a member, and myself placed our certificates in the Central Church, corner of Eighth and Cherry streets Dr Henry Steel Clark, Pastor

At this time, we resided on 11th street above Arch We remained members of the Central Church, until about the year 1859, and during this period I was active in Sunday School work

Having moved from 11th street to Green street, above 15th, in 1857, and finding the distance too great to Central Church.

We were induced to unite with other Presbyterians in that locality, in establishing a new church, which was organized in 1859, and called the Alexander Presbyterian Church, corner of 19th and Green streets, Dr Nevin, Pastor. The new enterprize greatly needing help, I gave all my energies for the success of the mission as Trustee, Treasurer, Teacher of the Sabbath School, and otherwise assisting in the work of the Mission After the erection of a temporary building, in less than one month, we withdrew our membership from the Central Church and joined the new enterprise In 1860 the church began to decline, owing to causes not necessary to state In the autumn of the same year, Dr Nevin resigned, leaving the church in the hands of the sheriff to be sold in three weeks At this juncture, I went to work and secured the funds to satisfy the mortgage, and thus the church was saved to the Presbytery. In about a year Dr Cunningham was

called to the Pastorate, and after he came, the church was put in working order We withdrew our membership, and went back to our old church home, corner of 8th and Cherry streets. At the same time we moved to 10th above Arch, quite near our Pastor, Dr. Clark, and the church, where we resided for some two or three years In the early part of the year 1864, Dr. Clark died The location not being a desirable one to live in, I purchased a house on North Broad Street, to which we moved in Oct, 1864.

Under my own personal supervision a mission Sabbath School was started and located near Broad and Oxford streets Having engaged the Rev John P Conkey, we commenced services in the Wagner Institute, but being somewhat out of the way of the population, we gave it up, and I hired a hall on Montgomery street, near 12th, but Mr. Conkey failing to give his energies and heart to the work, we had to give up the enterprise I then engaged in a new Mission School, on the corner of Broad and Oxford streets, and remained at work there, for four or five years, the result being that we organized a church called the *Oxford Church*, the pastor being Dr. Frank Robbins After building a fine church edifice in the fall of 1869 (though previously, I had withdrawn my certificate from the *Central Church* and joined the *Oxford Church*, also acting as trustee, and engaged as teacher in Sunday School, and other good works for strengthening the church), we moved to 3301 Arch street, West Philadelphia. On moving here, we joined Princeton

Church, Rev Dr Addison Henry, Pastor Here we remained for about three years, working in the Sabbath School, &c. My son, Albert, who was living on Cherry street near 20th at this time, attended the Second Church, corner 21st and Walnut, Dr Elias R. Beadle, Pastor. We then concluded to unite with this church, hoping our son would join with us in Christian fellowship I was elected Trustee, soon after Elder, also was a teacher in the Sabbath School until 1888.

JOHN GRAFF'S WILL

Dec 14th, 1818.

In the Name of God, Amen

I, John Graff, of Unity Township, Westmoreland Co., and State of Pennsylvania, Yeoman, being weak in body but of sound mind and memory and understanding, blessed be God for the same, but, considering the uncertainty of this transitory life, do make and publish this my last will and testament in manner and form following

Principally and first of all, I commend my immortal soul into the hands of Almighty God, who gave it, and as to such worldly estate wherewith it hath pleased God to bless me in this life, I give and dispose of the same in the following manner, viz I will that my beloved wife Barbara Graff, shall have the full use and possession of all my real and personal estate, until my youngest son is

arrived at full age. But should my beloved wife Barbara decease before my youngest son arrives to his full age, then my real and personal estate to fall into the hands of my three eldest sons, namely, Henry, William and John Graff, to do with it as they think proper, until my youngest son is arrived at his lawful age, and, after his arriving at lawful age, the place where I now live and reside, with the Coal Bank bought from Archibald McCallester, and one half of the Ridge place to be given unto my seven sons, namely, Henry, William, John, Peter, Jacob, Mathias and Paul Graff, at the valuation of Four Thousand Dollars, which sum is to be divided into eleven shares and four of said shares to be given unto my four daughters, share and share alike, namely, Polly Graff, now Polly Lose, Sarah, Margaret and Elizabeth Graff, to be given unto them or their lawful heirs or successors, at said time. But if my wife chooseth to change her way of living and marry, then she is to be paid four hundred dollars by my executors hereafter named, but if she continues my widow, she is to have the place called Poormans, with half the Ridge place to support her during her natural life, with as much stock and household furniture as she chooses to take without appraisement, and after her decease the place with half of the Ridge place to be given to my afore-named seven sons, or their lawful heirs or successors, for the sum of four thousand dollars, to be divided into eleven equal shares, to be given unto my aforesaid eleven children, share and share alike, or their lawful heirs or successors, and lastly I nominate, constitute and

appoint my beloved wife Barbara, Henry, William and John Graff, my three eldest sons, to be the sole executrix and executors of this my last will and testament, hereby revoking all other wills, legacies and bequests by me heretofore made, and declaring this and no other to be my last will and testament In witness whereof, I have hereto set my hand this fourteenth day of December, eighteen hundred and eighteen

Signed, sealed, published, pronounced and declared by the said testator as his last will and testament in the presence of us, who in the presence and at his request, have subscribed as witnesses.

JOHN GRAFF [SEAL]

WITNESSES.

MARTIN BASH,
ARCH'D McCALLISTER

Legally proven and recorded on the 20th day of July, 1824

ROBERT MONTGOMERY, Reg

GREENSBURG, WESTMORELAND CO

In memory of Father, Mother, Brothers and Sisters, what can I say sufficiently of such a Christian family

Shortly after the formation of our Government, father came to this country and married my mother, Barbara Baum, in 1793 At that time few people inhabited that

part of Westmoreland Co., in the State of Pennsylvania where all influences were more or less demoralizing to new settlers, such as Indian raids, murders, ungodliness, &c. Many of the settlers were uneducated, with no opportunity for improving their minds, such as schools and churches They were few in number, and great distances apart, and far from many homes—and these were about the only good influences in frontier life Nothing but the love of God in the hearts of my father and mother and continued Christian instruction could have exerted such influences on their children, so that when they grew up to man and womanhood, they developed such Christian characters and love for Christ, as they did.

First, there was Henry, the eldest, what a kind and generous brother he was, instructing and fitting the others for business in his own store, then giving them an interest in the business And so with John and Peter—that same spirit of generosity was developed as they grew in business qualifications and prospered in means—the earnest desire to assist others younger or older than themselves. The offer of giving assistance, and the keeping of worthy ones of the family in favorable positions, made a deep impression on my mind and heart To see father, brother or son in the same firm, showed the confidence and trust, towards one another also a manifestation, to my mind, that was both Christian and business like

And now a word for the sisters

Mary, the eldest sister, died in 1833 She was married and away from home, while I was yet a child, so I cannot

recall much concerning her, from my own recollection, but I have heard her son John, and others, speak of her kindness, and her lovely Christian character.

Sarah, the second sister, was a very hospitable Christian woman also kind and affectionate During camp meetings, many sisters in Christ found a welcome at her table

Margaret, the third sister, was a devoted Christian, early giving herself to the Lord, and joining the Presbyterian church, along with her husband She was kind and affectionate to all her brothers and sisters On her death-bed she prayed that she might see her brothers before dying.

Elizabeth, the fourth and youngest sister was a child of God early in life, a member of the M. E Church and a devoted follower of Christ. In her last sickness she suffered much, and, before her departure, she named all her brothers with her dying breath

And now, in conclusion, may the same spirit of Christian character, love and generosity, continue in the children, and the children's children, is my prayer

Anniversary of Marriage. *May 7th 1891*

ght of the family have lived to celebrate,

eir Fiftieth Marriage Anniversary.

nes as follows:-William over Fifty-five years.

m over Fifty-three years.

rgaret over Fifty-one years.

izabeth " Fifty-one years.

ter over Sixty years.

cob " Fifty years,

thew " Fifty-five years.

il " Fifty years.